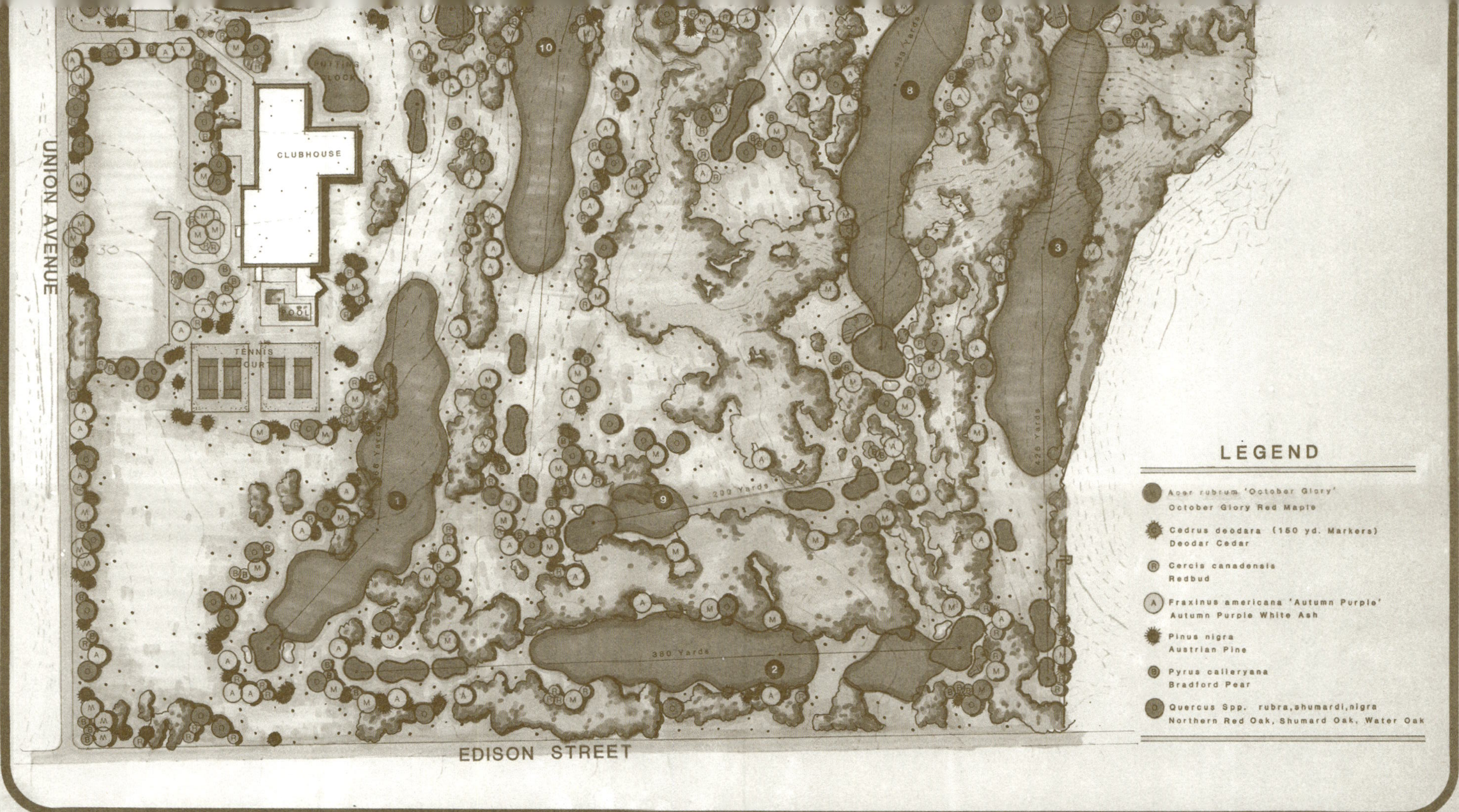

LANDSCAPE
PLANTING
PLAN
FOR

100' 0 25' 50' 100'

TULSA
· COUNTRY · CLUB ·
· tulsa · oklahoma ·

Golf Course Remodel By:

Jay Morrish and Associates, Ltd.
10820 East 45th Street Suite 101
Tulsa, OK 74146 918-665-2937

Landscape Master Plan By:

PLANNING DESIGN GROUP
Land Planning/Golf Course Architecture/Landscape Architecture
5155 East 51st Street, Suite 105, Tulsa, Oklahoma 74135 918-628-1255

BREAKING 100

Tulsa Country Club's First Century of Good Times and Good Friends

BREAKING 100

*Tulsa Country Club's First Century
of Good Times and Good Friends*

Randy Krehbiel

Copyright © 2009 by Tulsa Country Club

All rights reserved, including the right to reproduce this work in any form whatsoever without permission in writing from the publisher, except for brief passages in connection with a review. For information, please write:

The Donning Company Publishers
184 Business Park Drive, Suite 206
Virginia Beach, VA 23462

Steve Mull, General Manager
Barbara Buchanan, Office Manager
Pamela Koch, Senior Editor
Lori Wiley, Graphic Designer
Derek Eley, Imaging Artist
Cindy Smith, Project Research Coordinator
Tonya Hannink, Marketing Specialist
Pamela Engelhard, Marketing Advisor

Ed Williams, Project Director

Library of Congress Cataloging-in-Publication Data

Krehbiel, Randy.
    Breaking 100 : Tulsa Country Club's first century of good times and good friends / by Randy Krehbiel.
        p. cm.
    Includes bibliographical references and index.
    ISBN 978-1-57864-543-5 (hard cover : alk. paper)
    1. Tulsa Country Club (Oklahoma)—History. 2. Clubs—Oklahoma—Tulsa County—History. I. Title. II. Title: Breaking one hundred. III. Title: Breaking a hundred.
    HS2519.K74 2009
    367'.976686—dc22
                              2008051826

Printed in the United States of America at Walsworth Publishing Company

CONTENTS

Preface / 7

Chapter 1: **Teeing Off** / 9

Chapter 2: **Tillinghast** / 19

Chapter 3: **In the Rough** / 29

Chapter 4: **War and Peace** / 37

Chapter 5: **Bobby Sox Brigade** / 47

Chapter 6: **New Direction** / 57

Chapter 7: **Tulsa's Downtown Country Club** / 67

Chapter 8: **Staying the Course** / 75

Chapter 9: **Tillie's Ghost** / 83

Chapter 10: **Second Century** / 93

Appendix A: **Club Presidents** / 116

Appendix B: **TCC Course 1920–67** / 117

Appendix C: **Notable Tournaments at TCC** / 118

Appendix D: **Club Champions** / 119

Bibliography / 120

Photo Credits / 123

Index / 124

About the Author / 128

PREFACE

othing lasts one hundred years by accident. It takes some breaks, sure, but luck only goes so far. To last a hundred years takes work. Hard work. And that means somebody has to care.

A lot.

Tulsa Country Club has meant a lot to a lot of people since its founding in 1908. It has been a place of great joy—of lazy afternoons, good times with friends, wedding receptions and engagement parties—and, occasionally, of sorrow. The latter, thankfully, is most often the kind associated with hooked drives and dubbed putts.

It is not possible for something to survive a hundred years without it becoming an institution—that is, an integral part of its community.

Something, in fact, that both reflects its community and is out in front of it. Tulsa Country Club, it is safe to say, fits both requirements.

This book attempts to capture that interplay between the club and the community that nurtured it. The extent to which it succeeds is owed entirely to its members and staff, all of whom have been unfailingly helpful and generous with their time. Shortcomings are entirely the fault of the author.

Among those helping with this effort are general manager Jason Fiscus, head golf professional Jeff Combe, assistant manager Greg Holley, and club president David Thompson.

Among the membership, I would be remiss without specifically acknowledging Don Eustice, Forrest Shoemaker Jr., Jim Unruh, Dr. Mike Smith, Pat Cremin, Bob Kenney, Ron and Sonya Weese, Tom Chitwood, Rob Irwin, Paul Williams, Steve Stecher, Paul Sisemore, Tim Breedlove, A. B. Steen, Montie Box, and Phil Doherty. Others contributing their time and memories included Cleve Stubblefield, Harold Neal, Pat Gallagher, Eric Mueller, Buddy Phillips, Danna Sue Walker, Jim King, Blake Atkins, Tim Leslie, Dale McNamara, and Betsy Cullen. I would also like to acknowledge the assistance of the United States Golf Association, the Professional Golfers' Association, the Ladies Professional Golf Association, the Women's Oklahoma Golf Association, the Tillinghast Association, the *Tulsa World*, Rachele Vaughan, Hilary Pittman, Tom Gilbert, Ken MacLeod, Derek Hillman, the Tulsa City-County Library, John Fancher, the Tulsa Historical Society, and Howard Barnett.

And, of course, a special thanks to editor Pamela Koch and graphic designer Lori Wiley, without whom this book would never have made it to press.

A word about sources. This book draws on a wide variety of sources, including books, periodicals, personal interviews, and club archives. Local newspapers—the *Tulsa World*, *Tulsa Tribune*, and *Tulsa Democrat*—were the leading primary sources for historical information about the club and events in Tulsa. Historical quotations are from the *Tulsa World* unless otherwise noted.

A far cry from today's lush landscape, the Tulsa Country Club course originally doubled as a dairy pasture and had earlier been used to hold cattle awaiting shipment on the nearby Frisco Railroad. In this photo, a party of golfers can be seen in the distance.

CHAPTER ONE

Teeing Off

H. P. Anderson had seen golf but not actually played it when he decided Tulsa needed a course.

He had been introduced to the sport in Los Angeles, which by 1900 already had several courses. Anderson himself had little time for the game then. He operated a small grocery store, and his customers included some wildcatters who, in keeping with what was already oilfield tradition, paid for their beans and coffee with more promises than cash. So Anderson took shares of production as credit against their bill; when they hit it big, he did, too.

Anderson moved to Tulsa shortly after, bought an ice business and kept his hand in oil, and rounded up a surprising number of like-minded souls intrigued by the idea of chasing a little ball around the prairie. Although golf had not taken hold in the United States until the mid-1880s, the country counted more than one thousand golf courses in 1900. That same year, the first two courses in what is now Oklahoma were laid out in Guthrie and Oklahoma City.

Anderson and his friends opened theirs in June 1905. Tulsa Country Club, as they called it, included a nine-hole course, a clubhouse, tennis courts, and a shooting range on eighty leased acres southeast of Tulsa, near the present-day Hillcrest Medical Center.

A variation of the story is that oilmen from the East brought golf and the country club phenomenon—another trend sweeping the nation—to Tulsa. Either way, oil figured into the equation—just as it figured into about everything else that happened in and around Tulsa in those years and the years that followed.

Tulsa of 1905 was not yet the oil capital of the world. It wasn't even the largest town in Indian Territory. Or the second largest. Tulsa was just a modest town of a few thousand residents, no paved streets, and not much else in the way of amenities. But it was ambitious and growing, with three rail lines running through it and aspirations of surpassing Muskogee as the major metropolis of Indian Territory. That year the Tulsa Commercial Club—forerunner of the Chamber of Commerce—chartered a special train to the east to promote the town. Among the emissaries was one Bill Rogers, a trick roper destined to find fame as the humorist and entertainer Will Rogers. The trip was such a success that several more were undertaken in future years, one of them featuring the old bank robber Emmett Dalton.

No, Tulsa was not yet the oil capital of the world in June 1905—but there was oil, if not in Tulsa, at least all around it. The weekly *Indian Republican* newspaper reported 211 well completions in the territory during April 1905; 158 of them were producers. In July, the Cleveland field, west of Tulsa and just inside Oklahoma Territory, pumped eleven thousand barrels a day.

This was enough to start the migration: from Pennsylvania, Ohio, Indiana, and Kansas, and even from New York. The Pennsylvania influence was particularly notable; western Pennsylvania had been the cradle of the American petroleum industry, and many of those who found their way to Tulsa had started in or passed through Pittsburgh. And, it so happened, one of America's first great country club golf courses had opened just outside of Pittsburgh, at Oakmont, in 1903.

In truth, most of those hacking the ball around Tulsa's nine-hole course probably knew very little about golf. The club's landlord, an Indian woman named Clarissa Bell, became so annoyed by the stray balls flying past and against her house on a corner of the property that she collected them at gunpoint and refused to surrender them.

Still, a good time seems to have been had by all. The October 1905 *Sturm's Statehood Magazine*, a territorial publication based in Tulsa, featured a full-page photo of "Mrs. M.C. Hale of Tulsa, I.T.," swinging a golf club as part of a story lauding "Recreation in Indian Territory." Visitors from the East, the author says, are surprised to learn "the tennis racquet and driver better suited to his needs" than a sidearm, and that he is more likely to hear "tee off" than "hands up."

Nevertheless, gunshots seem to have been more common than golf shots on the country club grounds.

"Marksmen were in the majority," reported *Sturm's*, "a few had played lawn tennis or read of golf."

The clubhouse cost $1,500, not an insignificant sum in those days, and featured electric lights powered by a spring water–driven generator. The golf course measured 2,306 yards, with the shortest hole 133 yards and the longest, 384. Bogey—"par" didn't become the standard until around 1911—was 43.

According to stories that fall in the *Tulsa World* and *Tulsa Democrat*, twenty players entered the first city championship—a series of matches played over a period of about six weeks. Scores in the

A pioneer Tulsa physician, Dr. Samuel Grant Kennedy gave up medicine to concentrate on investments in oil and real estate. In 1908 he leased about eighty acres to the newly formed Tulsa Country Club for its golf course. TCC continued leasing its course from the Kennedy family until 1958.

60s and 70s for nine holes were common, and at least one score in the 90s was recorded. Dr. W. A. Cook—"considered to be one of the best golf players in the southwest," according to the October 23, 1905, *Democrat*—was the eventual winner despite being absent "for several weeks . . . visiting home folks in Iowa."

Just weeks later, while drilling on the Glenn farm twelve miles southwest of Tulsa, an oil prospector named Bob Galbreath heard what he later described as a chuckling sound deep in the ground. Within seconds, oil shot out of the hole and above the top of the derrick, signaling the start of a new era for Tulsa and the soon-to-be state of Oklahoma. Within months, the Glenn Pool was producing more oil than the entire state of Texas, and the future of Tulsa—if not the first Tulsa Country Club—was assured.

The first Tulsa Country Club lasted about a year. Why it did not last longer is unclear.

"The club has 60 members, and the number still increases," reported the *Tulsa Democrat* of January 24, 1906. Perhaps a more profitable use for the land was found. Perhaps Clarissa Bell got tired of fending off wayward golf balls. At any rate, by the end of 1906, the club had been dissolved and the clubhouse turned into a private residence.

But country clubs were rapidly becoming a necessary accouterment for any American city or town of ambition, and by late October 1907, talk of a new country club catering to young oilmen had made its way into the *Tulsa World*. Plans included a golf course and a clubhouse to be used "principally as a loafing place for the members." The following March, "a number of Tulsa's sportsmen" incorporated a new country club "of the highest type, although not such a high-class one as will keep the man of moderate means away."

Four men—Matt Taylor, E. Rogers Kemp, Frank L. Moore, and R. W. Kellough—signed incorporation papers dated March 18, 1908. The documents were received by the secretary of state's office in Oklahoma City eight days later, on March 26. Two hundred shares in the club were sold for fifty dollars each to capitalize the enterprise.

Some rolling pastureland on the northwest edge of town was leased from Dr. Samuel Grant Kennedy and his wife Agnes, a member of the Osage Nation. The tract, just inside what had been the Osage Reservation and was now Osage County, is generally described as being eighty acres, although the lease itself is not specific. A Missouri native and pioneer Tulsan, Samuel Kennedy and his brother James (also a doctor) had married sisters of French-Osage extraction. Through them and their children, a sizeable parcel of the former Osage land passed into Kennedy hands. The country club set on part of Agnes Lombard Kennedy's anticipated allotment, an expectation not fully realized until 1909, her son Jim later said.

Although Samuel Kennedy himself doesn't seem to have been a golfer, his seven children were. Son Jim would win four state amateur titles and start Tulsa's first public golf course. His brothers Lee and Sam Jr. were also good amateurs, and sister Ann was among the best women in the state.

The new Tulsa Country Club was completely separate from its predecessor but included many of the former club's members, among them H. P. Anderson, Harold Rose, A. C. Houck, G. T. Williamson, E. F. Hannon, and Wallace Campbell. Other prominent Tulsans among the founding

Main Street Tulsa, looking north, in 1908, the year Tulsa Country Club was founded. Modern Tulsa began as a small railhead settlement in 1882. A Tulsa post office had been established a few years earlier at a ranch house near present-day Forty-first Street and Yorktown Avenue. An earlier Creek Indian settlement around the Council Oak at present-day Eighteenth Street and Cheyenne Avenue was abandoned during the American Civil War.

members included E. Rogers Kemp, H. Y. "Cap" Arnold, Cyrus Avery, Tate Brady, J. E. Crosbie, R. L. Davidson, A. L. Farmer, L. J. Martin, John Mitchell, C. L. Reeder, H. C. Tyrell, P. J. White, and Charles J. Wrightsman.

According to a typed membership list dating from that era, F. A. Leovy was the club's first president. J. A. Steel served as vice president and J. H. Yust as treasurer. A *Tulsa World* story from April 25, 1908, however, says Kemp was the first president, Leovy vice president, and Lewis Emery Jr. secretary-treasurer.

The two sources also disagree on the first board of directors. The newspaper story named Kemp, Leovy, Williamson, Anderson, Wrightsman, John A. Steel, Robert Oglesby, Manuel Hirsch, and J. S. Glenn. The typed list differs by including H. C. Ashby, F. K. L. Moore, and E. R. Perry while leaving off Hirsch, Glenn, and Wrightsman.

A foursome tees off during Tulsa Country Club's early days.

The course's first putting surfaces were made of oil mixed with sand.

The *World* story said membership was to be limited to one hundred, with eighty "of the most prominent business and professional men of the city" already pledged. The tract, it continued, "was evidently designed for the purpose it has been secured by the local sportsmen."

A local architect has prepared plans for the clubhouse, which is to be a large and well-arranged building, and contractors will be asked for bids for its construction in a few days.

A force of men has been busy several days working on the grounds, which will be

The 1916 clubhouse as seen from the west.

in shape for use in two weeks at the most. There will be a nine-hole golf course, tennis course [*sic*] and shooting range.

Country clubs began appearing in the East in the mid-1880s, at about the same time that golf began to take hold. Several factors, including urbanization and the growing number of men in occupations that kept them cooped up in offices all day, contributed to the popularity of both. Some clubs included other activities, including tennis, bowling, fox hunting, and even horse racing, but golf soon emerged as the favorite of the country club set.

Early on, all golf equipment had to be imported into the United States, which made it almost prohibitively expensive. But A. G. Spalding & Company began selling American-made clubs in 1894, and three years later, Dayton Last Company, which made wooden lasts for shoes, began turning out persimmon heads. Dayton Last soon gave up the shoe business to make sporting goods equipment under the name MacGregor Golf.

Another development during these years also nurtured American interest in golf. An Ohio businessman named Coburn Haskell developed the first wound rubber ball, called the "Bouncing Billy" because of its liveliness. Gutta Percha, the standard for half a century, remained popular for a while longer, but once manufacturers learned to bring the Bouncing Billies under control with aerodynamic dimples, the wound rubber ball's longer carry revolutionized the game.

The new Tulsa Country Club clubhouse opened on June 23, 1908, according to a note in the club's archives. Whether the golf course was open for play in early May, as the *Tulsa World* story predicted, is not known. Jim Kennedy remembered six holes with sand putting surfaces opening before the other three. Certainly the course was in use, if not finished, by late summer. So were the tennis courts.

A crowd has turned out to watch this early match at the club. This photo may have been taken during the first state tournaments, held at TCC in 1910.

"Society and athletic people of Tulsa are looking forward with much anticipation to the Golf Tournament to be given at the Country Club Saturday afternoon," reported the Thursday, September 3 *Tulsa Democrat*. The "scratch" tournament, it explained, would be used to handicap subsequent tournaments planned for the remainder of the fall and winter.

A tennis tournament, the *Democrat* went on to say, was planned for the following weekend.

"This is the beginning of many good things for those interested in athletic sports," the newspaper predicted.

Alas, Tulsa golfers were not as proficient as they perhaps believed. In late September, a Muskogee Town and Country Club team "played gentle ringlets" around a visiting TCC contingent. Stung by defeat, the Tulsans did what losing teams often do—they hired the other team's coach.

Thus did one "W. Nichols" become TCC's first golf pro, if only on a temporary basis. The September 30, 1908, *Tulsa World* announced Nichols, who had so ably directed the Muskogee golfers, would be available "every afternoon this week except Saturday [for] an exhibition of the noble sport." The newspaper assured its readers that, despite his suspect surname, Nichols was indeed a true Scotsman "whose 'mither' was a McGregor."

Nichols had also been engaged to finish laying out the nine-hole golf course, which apparently had not yet been completed.

"Our local golf artists will work strenuously, for they liketh not positions . . . in the rear guard," said the *World*.

Coincidentally, more than eighty years later, Nichols's grandson Jim King would serve as president of Tulsa Country Club.

In 1909, country club members from Oklahoma City, Shawnee, Muskogee, and Tulsa met at TCC to form the Oklahoma Golf Association. The organization's first state championship was scheduled for the following spring on the country club course.

Welcoming the players was a front-page cartoon in the May 23, 1910, *Tulsa Democrat*, featuring a bowlegged fellow in plaid plus fours and golf shoes adorned by spurs. His golfing ensemble also included a broad sombrero, bandana, six-shooter and gun-belt, western-style cavalry gauntlets, a golf club, and a shaggy moustache. The anti-Republican newspaper also managed to work in an unflattering caricature of rotund, golf-loving President William Howard Taft.

The tournament began the next day with a single thirty-six-hole match between the only two professionals entered, Oklahoma City Lakeside Country Club's Leslie Brownlee and Muskogee Town and Country Club's William Nichols—the same "W. Nichols" whose "mither" was a "McGregor."

It wasn't much of a match. Nichols led 8-up after eighteen holes when Brownlee conceded. Thus

Nichols went into the books as the winner of the first Oklahoma Open, now the nation's second oldest continuously played state open.

The thirty-two amateurs entered played an eighteen-hole qualifying round the following day. C. F. Moore of Muskogee posted the low score for the day, an 87. W. M. Armstrong's 100 was the best for a Tulsan.

Muskogee Town and Country Club swept all three amateur flights, with only one Tulsan making the finals. Despite the locals' disappointing showing, the *Tulsa World* called the tournament "successful in every way and highly enjoyed by those participating." The *World* admitted the course was not in the best condition but asserted, "some very good scores were made."

But the *Democrat*'s Glenn Condon, Tulsa's first sportswriter and later sports editor of both the short-lived *Tulsa Post* and the *Tulsa World*, complained of the tournament's "low scores," by which he apparently meant high scores.

"The scores that were made in the three days [sic] tournament which closed yesterday were very very low [sic] and bear a decidedly 'beginnerish' tinge," he reported. "Some of the participating players attribute this to the condition of the course at the country club. Experts say that the course is one of the finest in the state."

Muskogee's Harry Gwinnup defeated E. R. Perry of Tulsa for the A flight championship despite the fact "Gwinnup's card doesn't show any very great work," according to the *Democrat*'s peevish commentary.

Then, in perhaps a tongue-in-cheek display of homerism, the writer added: "Perry's playing, of course, is not to be criticized."

Tulsa was by now a booming oil town with a population approaching twenty thousand in the 1910 census—a tenfold increase in just twelve years. It had proudly added an institution of higher learning, Henry Kendall College, whose football prowess would spark a movement to change the school's name in 1921 to the University of Tulsa. The city also claimed the world's first "oilman's bank," known today as the Bank of Oklahoma.

But Tulsa was still in most ways a small town, and that included the country club. It was

This cartoon on the front page of the Tulsa Democrat *welcomed golfers to the first state championships, held at TCC in May 1910. Harry Gwinnup, then of Muskogee and later of TCC, won the amateur title. Only two players entered the open tournament, with William Nichols of Muskogee declared the winner when his opponent withdrew. Eighty-six years later, Nichols's grandson Jim King served as TCC president.*

Tulsa's fire department was the first west of the Mississippi to become fully motorized. This photo of the department and all of its equipment was taken in front of the TCC clubhouse about 1920.

only about a mile from the city's center but a true "country" club nonetheless. The clubhouse sat at the end of a lane winding through an orchard, and livestock roamed the grounds. This in itself was not unusual; many clubs used goats or sheep to keep the grass down in the days before mechanized mowers. But Tulsa Country Club's four-legged groundskeepers were Homer Kennedy's Holsteins.

"Golfers had to keep a wary eye out for range bulls and my cousin's dairy cattle," Jim Kennedy recalled in a 1964 interview with the *Tulsa Tribune*'s Bob Foresman.

The holes were identified by name rather than number and carried such colorful sobriquets as "Westward Ho" and "Profanity Creek." Other activities included bridge, which was becoming increasingly popular nationally as well as in Tulsa. Several tournaments a week were scheduled, and were a way of getting women more involved in the club— somewhat to the dismay, it must be said, of some of the men.

The clubhouse is remembered as not much more than a log cabin, although it seems to have been updated several times and completely refurnished in 1915. A probably not entirely objective report in the *Tulsa Democrat* described it, following the 1915 sprucing, as "the most attractive building of its kind in the state." By the mid-teens, the clubhouse was deemed sufficiently civilized to routinely host the type of event reported in the *Democrat*'s February 1, 1916, society column:

Miss Dorothy Madison and her fiancé, Mr. Winston P. Henry, were beautifully honored last evening by Messrs. J. A. Glamman and R. W. McIntosh, who were hosts at a handsome dinner-dance at the Country club in ante-nuptial courtesy to the two popular young society folk.

A Valentine's Day dance was scheduled for a few days later, but an electrical fire early on February 2 destroyed the clubhouse. No one was injured, but 150 sets of golf clubs did perish in the conflagration.

Clubhouse fires, especially electrical fires, seem to have been common throughout the United States during these years. In many cases, the fires were accepted with more rejoicing than grief because they often allowed clubs to replace outdated and outgrown facilities with new and modern ones.

Tulsa Country Club members may not have been overjoyed to lose their old cabin—they carried only $5,500 in insurance on a building valued at $10,000—but they reacted resolutely. "Country Club to rebuild at once," the *Tulsa World* headline read one day after the fire. "Magnificent structure to arise from embers of the old one."

According to an unsigned note in the TCC archives, club president Cap Arnold favored a modest structure, but some of the younger members "got busy and had a big proxy hunt" to push through a more ambitious building program.

The club's capital stock had been increased from $10,000 to $30,000 in 1914 and was raised again to $50,000 after the fire. In June, work began on a $50,000 clubhouse that would be Tulsa Country Club's home for the next fifty years. It opened the following February to great fanfare:

DEPT. 1920

With the opening of the new country club house northwest of the city tomorrow night, one of the most complete club houses in the entire southwest will be ready for occupation. The house is complete in every way. It consists of locker rooms, a room for golf equipment, grill room, banquet hall, restroom, bowling alleys, parlors, halls and a billiard room....

The building proper is a rambling three-story dull red brick-colored stone trimmed structure sitting on the top of [a] grassy knoll. Beyond the house is the shallow straggling creek, sparsely wooded, designed principally to infuse adjectives into the speech of golfers.

Tulsa World
February 18, 1917

The basement contained locker rooms, a grill, bowling lanes, and a sort of early-day pro shop where clubs were repaired and "manufactured." The first floor, the *World* said, "represents the last word in luxurious clubhouse furnishings," with oak floors and walls covered in "deep mottled blue paper." The furniture, the *World* continued, was the "'na-plus-ultra' of parlor furniture." A giant painting of wood nymphs "bearing the unmistakable marks of genius" provided a backdrop to a ballroom with "one of the finest floors in the city." The second story included a balcony overlooking the ballroom and a billiard room with four tables.

In May, a *World* society column item announced: "Last week's dinner-dance of the country club proved such a delightful innovation that plans have been made for a similar affair Friday evening."

The grounds were extensively renovated. "Large cement gateways" now welcomed members and their guests. Roadways were paved and three clay tennis courts built north of the clubhouse. According to the *World*, the improvements totaled $250,000 to $300,000.

The club wasn't finished, either. Just before the clubhouse opening, officers announced a complete reworking of the golf course at a cost of another $30,000 to $50,000. Historically, golf courses had no standard number of holes. The venerable St. Andrews had, at one time, twenty-two. The earliest U.S. courses had only three or four. By 1917, though, eighteen was becoming the accepted norm. For Tulsa in general, and Tulsa Country Club in particular, only the most up-to-date of everything was acceptable.

William M. Langford, a Chicago landscape architect who laid out some of the upper Midwest's early courses and who, with partner T. J. Moreau, would design some 250 courses in his career, was hired to build a new course in Tulsa.

"Every hole on the present course will be abandoned," reported the May 1, 1917, *World*. "Part of the property will be surrendered and the new links will be more rectangular than that now in use."

Apparently, the course was extended to eighteen holes but did not meet the club's expectations. Less than three years later, it decided to completely redesign the course and add about five hundred yards in length. Only this time, the job went to one of golf's most colorful and enduring personalities.

A. W. Tillinghast, shown here going over the survey for a proposed course in Texas, stumbled onto his career as a golf architect when some friends asked him to help lay one out in Pennsylvania in 1909.

CHAPTER TWO

Tillinghast

He was known as "Tillie the Terror" and "The Mad Master." He could be temperamental and arrogant, charming and candid. He loved a good stiff drink and a story well told. And he was a genius.

During a twenty-five-year span beginning in 1911, Albert Warren Tillinghast created from scratch or redesigned perhaps 120 golf courses—no one knows the exact number—including some of the greatest in the game. Among Tillinghast's courses was Tulsa Country Club's.

Tillinghast was near the height of his popularity when, on March 30, 1920, he signed a one-page contract to redesign the Tulsa Country Club course for a fee of $2,000. Probably, he had already examined the course extensively. According to one source, he visited it in 1919 with Charles "Chick" Evans, the 1916 U.S. Open and U.S. Amateur champion and one of only two men—Bobby Jones being the other—to win both tournaments in the same year. Some sources from the 1950s say Tillinghast was the course's original designer, but this seems unlikely. Tillinghast didn't lay out his first course until 1909 and didn't become a full-time architect until a year or two after that.

Unfortunately, there is no record of the exact work undertaken by Tillinghast in 1920, except that it was so extensive the state's top players were invited to the club in September of that year to reacquaint themselves with the course ahead of the state amateur and open tournaments. On April 7, shortly after the contract with Tillinghast was signed, the *Tulsa Tribune* (successor to the old *Democrat*) reported: "Plans, which are at present in a tentative state, call for additional yardage of 500 to 600 yards but will remain an 18-hole course. However, it will be [so] completely rearranged that it will be practically unknown."

If "rearrangement" is what Tulsa Country Club wanted, it went to the right man. Just two years earlier, Baltusrol Golf Club in Springfield, New Jersey, had hired Tillinghast to build a second course to complement an eighteen-hole

A facsimile of the letter sent Tulsa Country Club by A. W. Tillinghast, confirming his arrangement with the club for rebuilding the club's golf course. Tillinghast was to receive a total of $4,000 for the job.

layout that had already hosted two U.S. Opens and a half-dozen or so other national tournaments. Tillinghast persuaded the club to plow up the existing course and build two new ones instead.

Golf historian Frank Hannigan, who reawakened interest in Tillinghast with a 1974 article in *The Golf Journal*, writes: "A. W. Tillinghast is the forgotten genius of American golf. He was as accomplished in the various crafts and sub-cultures in our insular world of golf as any American before or since. At the same time, he was one of the wildest and most outlandish figures in the game's history."

As an architect, Tillinghast subscribed to the notion that "A round of golf should present 18 inspirations." He immersed himself in a piece of ground before laying out a course so that the course fit the contours of land. Tillinghast enthusiasts Stephen Goodwin and Rick Wolfe write that he relied "on the inspiration of the moment to fashion the details of each hole as it emerged from the landscape."

Tillinghast's common practice, they continue, "was to seat himself in the shade of a tree, bottle in hand, and call out directions to his workmen as they shaped the course with their mule-pulled scoops."

Golf architect and historian Geoffrey S. Cornish, in the introduction to one of the collections of Tillinghast's essays, describes Tillie as a "determined artist" who "used the site, not the drawing board, as his canvas."

Born into an affluent Philadelphia family in 1874, Tillinghast lived a troublesome youth and dissolute early manhood notable primarily for his high living and intense interest in golf. A good but not great golfer, he traveled frequently to Scotland and seems to have known—and photographed— all of the game's leading personalities from the

A. W. Tillinghast, right, goes over plans with an unidentified job foreman. Tillinghast believed in personally overseeing every aspect of the work on his courses.

1890s onward. Tillinghast was among the first to recognize the ability of a young Bobby Jones and claimed to have been present the first time the word "birdie" was used to denote playing a hole one stroke under par.

In 1909, Tillinghast agreed to help some friends lay out a course at Shawnee-on-the-Delaware in easternmost Pennsylvania. Except for his experience as a player, Tillinghast had no real qualifications for the job, but the course was well received when it opened two years later, and Tillinghast was soon working furiously. He tended to favor subtlety over brute strength; torturous little par threes were his specialty.

"A closely guarded green," Tillinghast wrote, "is the surest test of any man's golf."

Tillinghast's work at Tulsa Country Club involved more than rearranging the holes. He also converted the putting surfaces from sand greens—an oxymoron if ever there was one—to grass. As the name implies, sand greens were simply raked sand (or, sometimes, compressed cottonseed) mixed with oil. Sediment from the bottom of storage tanks was said to work best. Naturally, these surfaces were extraordinarily slow by modern standards and susceptible to "doctoring," either to make putts easier or harder.

Thus, the new "green" greens proved quite a challenge. An October 10, 1921, headline over a story about the annual club tournament announced: "Nine New Grass Greens Are Hard For All Contestants."

"Those nine new grass greens . . . proved exceedingly difficult," wrote *Tulsa World* sports editor B. A. Bridgewater. "Nearly everybody required more strokes for the new nine than for the nine sand greens."

Runner-up Flint Moss must have been particularly aggrieved. He required a nine on the seventh hole on his way to a still-respectable 80. Defending state amateur champion Jim Kennedy managed a 77.

Despite the difficulties, the new course was received enthusiastically. The tournament attracted 110 entries, a record.

"Not only was the entry list larger than ever before, but most of those starting finished and turned in cards instead of quitting when they got far behind," wrote Bridgewater.

Tillinghast spent parts of at least two and perhaps three or even four summers in Tulsa. The TCC course was largely rebuilt by late 1920, but the grass greens weren't finished until two years later. In one of his many essays on golf, Tillinghast mentions being in Tulsa during the 1921 race riot. Tillinghast was also building what is now The Oaks Country Club course during this period; in another of his essays, Tillinghast says that job took several years because of difficulties clearing titles to the necessary land.

Tillinghast, in the form of a wood sculpture alongside the first fairway, still overlooks Tulsa Country Club. His vision was somewhat disturbed in the mid-1960s when a new clubhouse was built across the course from the old one, necessitating a reordering and in some cases realigning of the holes. Twenty years later, in the 1980s, designer Jay Morrish was brought in to restore the Tillinghast feel. Morrish completely replaced three holes and reworked several others.

"I don't know how many people remember Tillinghast or what his courses looked like," Morrish said in a 1988 *Tulsa World* story. "But I hope people will still give him credit for this course."

A. W. Tillinghast wasn't the only colorful character in Tulsa during the summer of 1920. Earlier that year, on the recommendation of Chick Evans, the club had hired a twenty-two-year-old professional from Chicago named William E. Mehlhorn, known then as "Bill" or even more commonly as "Billy." Tillinghast's introduction to him, described in one of Tillinghast's essays, left a lasting impression on the famous architect.

> My attention was attracted by a solitary man who had been swinging an iron for an hour, and was still swinging it, in fact, out on a flat hillside. Far across the slight valley was a caddy retrieving ball after ball, and he was not even working up a sweat for he seldom had to move far out of his tracks. On this hillside was spread a pocket handkerchief, the target at which the iron shots

were being directed, and the balls fell about this small square of white with monotonous regularity. . . .

If it happened that two or three successive shots did stray a bit wide of the mark, the distant figure displayed every symptom of utter disgust.

After observing this for a second straight day, Tillinghast inquired of the local accompanying him, "Who is that bird over there?"

After divulging Mehlhorn's identity, Tillinghast's companion said, "He must have hit a million balls over at the rag."

The club's first full-time pro had been an amiable Scot named Art Jackson. Arriving in 1912 and staying three years, Jackson wound up in Oklahoma City, where he built and was for years head pro of the Lincoln Park public courses and was instrumental in developing the state's junior program. Mehlhorn's predecessor—and, as it turned out, successor—was the popular J. C. "Jock" Collins, whose son Joe later played for the University of Tulsa.

Mehlhorn was a scrapper, below average height and build but sinewy, with a square jaw and protruding ears. He had grown up in the Chicago suburbs of Elgin and Glencoe, laying bricks alongside his German immigrant father. At ten, Mehlhorn began caddying at Skokie Country Club for thirty cents a round; at sixteen, he quit school to become assistant pro at thirty dollars a month.

Largely self-taught, Mehlhorn had already won several smaller tournaments when he arrived in Tulsa. He had tied for seventeenth in the 1919 PGA Championship, and was beginning to acquire the reputation for shot-making that would earn him the nickname "Wild Bill."

Ambitious and outgoing, Mehlhorn quickly went to work drumming up business for the club—and himself.

"William 'Billy' Mehlhorn, of Chicago, new professional of the Tulsa Country Club, is not only

Young and ambitious, with a flair for self-promotion, Bill Mehlhorn made a big impression during his short stay in Tulsa. TCC's pro for about six months during the summer of 1920, he finished ninth in the PGA Championship and made a run at the U.S. Open before faltering in the final round.

a crack golfer, he's a great little organizer," the *Tulsa World* announced on March 14, 1920. "'Billy' had not been in town two days before there was a noticeable increase in the number of golfers on the greens of the club."

That summer, Mehlhorn tied for ninth in the PGA Championship and flirted with the upper echelons of the U.S. Open before fading to twenty-seventh. He submitted pieces to the *Tulsa Tribune*, earning at least one byline, and broke the Tulsa Country Club course record for nine holes with a 32.

By the fall, Mehlhorn had moved on. Years later, in an interview with author Al Barkow, he said it was because the course was torn up all summer.

"All I could do was hit balls and give a few lessons," he said.

From 1923 through 1930, Mehlhorn was among the game's top professionals. He won twenty tour events and in 1921 played on the first American international team. He was a member of the first U.S. Ryder Cup team. He shot a 32 on the front nine on the last day of the 1927 U.S. Open and a 65—while dead drunk, according to Mehlhorn—on the last day of the 1930 Western Open. For a while, he held the record for the lowest seventy-two-hole score in a PGA event.

Tillinghast thought Mehlhorn might become one of the all-time greats. Ben Hogan said he was the best player he ever saw from tee to green. But Mehlhorn couldn't putt. Jokingly, he blamed the heavy work he did as a boy for ruining his touch. Whatever the case, his short game kept Mehlhorn from winning a major championship and reaching the sport's upper strata.

But Mehlhorn did become one of the game's great teachers. Setting up shop in Florida, he remained an active coach until his death in 1989 at the age of ninety.

The third star in Tulsa Country Club's orbit that summer of 1920 was not so transient. He had, in fact, grown up alongside the course and would live next to it the rest of his life.

The first of Sam and Agnes Kennedy's seven children, Jim Kennedy was born in 1898 in a five-room house at the corner of Fourth Street and Boston Avenue where an office building bearing the family name still stands. Within a few years, the Kennedy clan had moved onto Agnes Kennedy's Osage allotment northwest of downtown. When the club opened in 1908, Jim Kennedy became a member of the original caddie corps. Soon, he was playing.

"I was fortunate enough to have enough money and time to play golf," Kennedy recalled in a 1976 interview with the *Tulsa World*, "Not many people played back in those days. I didn't tell anyone in high school that I played golf because it was a sissy sport back then."

In 1920, just past his twenty-second birthday, Kennedy entered both the state amateur and an open tournament played the same week at Tulsa Country Club.

Bill Mehlhorn (front row, second from left) played on the first U.S. Ryder Cup team in 1927. The rest of the team: (front row, from left) Leo Diegel, Mehlhorn, Walter Hagen, Al Espinosa, Gene Sarazen; (second row) Johnny Golden, Joe Turnesa, Johnny Farrell, Al Waltrous.

A threesome, with caddies, circa 1925.

On October 18, a Sunday, Kennedy shot a thirty-six-hole 152 to tie Mehlhorn for medalist in the open qualifying. On Monday, Kennedy played eighteen holes, and though his game was a little off, he qualified for the championship flight of the state amateur. On Tuesday, he won two matches, 7-and-5 and 7-and-6, and on Wednesday beat C. W. Bass of Tulsa 8-and-7, in the semifinals.

That set up a final with four-time state champion Harry Gwinnup, who had moved from Muskogee to Tulsa and become a TCC member. Kennedy won, 4-and-3.

"Veteran golf experts of Oklahoma . . . agree that yesterday's match was the best ever played in a title round," wrote the *Tulsa World*'s Larry Dailey.

"Kennedy owes his victory to faultless putting and long and accurate driving, the latter especially," Dailey continued. "He was seldom in trouble off the tees, while Gwinnup frequently drove into roughs."

Kennedy and Mehlhorn were to have had an eighteen-hole playoff for the open title on Sunday, two days after the amateur final, but the course was deemed "not in condition for championship play." Instead, Mehlhorn, Kennedy, and Jock Collins played an eighteen-hole exhibition on Saturday. On his ninth round of competitive golf in seven days, the weary Kennedy shot 83, ten shots behind Collins and five behind Mehlhorn.

The amateur title was the first of four in a row for Kennedy. In 1923, he built a house in the family compound only a nine-iron from the clubhouse and lived there the rest of his life. He quit playing golf in the mid-1930s for medical reasons, but took up big game hunting with his wife Verva. In the 1950s, the couple sponsored the National Turkey Calling Championship trophy.

Kennedy was an important figure in Midwestern golf throughout the 1920s, and his correspondence with Chick Evans and others offers a glimpse into the game as it was in that era. He opened the city's first public course in 1925, adjacent to the country club; the first four holes, in fact, were east of Union Avenue on land now part of the club. An honorary lifetime member of Tulsa Country Club, Kennedy worked out the terms by which the club finally acquired its course from the family trust in the 1950s.

James A. Kennedy, pictured here in later life, lived almost his entire life next door to Tulsa Country Club. Starting as a caddie in 1908, he became a top-flight amateur in the 1920s and had his own private entrance onto the golf course. The gate can still be seen near the third tee.

In the 1970s, near the end of his life, Kennedy shared a barber with Jim Unruh, a Tulsa lawyer and TCC president. They often bumped into each other while getting their hair cut, and on one such occasion, Kennedy handed over a box containing a trove of club memorabilia, including his bronze lifetime membership card, correspondence dating back to the 1920s, and copies of the club's by-laws from its very earliest days. He was, in essence, passing the torch.

Jim Kennedy died in 1979 at the age of eighty.

Tulsa of the 1920s was called the Magic City. The 1920 census counted 72,000 inhabitants, four times the 1910 population, and that probably understated the true number. For one thing, it did not take into consideration thousands of people living outside the city limits but who were Tulsans for all intents and purposes. The corporate boundaries covered only thirteen square miles, extending only to Twenty-first Street on the south, barely crossing the Arkansas River on the west and ending about a half-mile from the Frisco Railroad tracks to the north. To the east, the city limits reached as far as Lewis Avenue in some places. Communities with such names as Dawson, Bruner Station, and Hickory had not yet been absorbed by the ameba-like sprawl that would soon subsume them into modern Tulsa.

Rents and real estate values skyrocketed. The city's skyline took shape, causing Tulsa to tout itself as the "Metropolis of Oklahoma." In 1924, the Treasury Department reported twice as many tax returns in the top income bracket from Tulsa County as any other county in the state. That same year, the Census Bureau estimated Tulsa's population to be in excess of 111,000, making it the state's largest city.

There were, to be sure, less attractive aspects of this growth. Refinery and oil field workers, clustered mainly west of the Arkansas River, often lived in abject poverty. A squalid red light district, replete with illegal gin joints and cheap hotels fronting brothels, lined the streets adjacent to the railroad tracks. And, the 1921 race riot killed dozens and left thousands homeless.

But there was no escaping Tulsa's sense of destiny and pride. Radio, in the form of William G. Skelly's KVOO, arrived. The first municipal airport was built and, for a brief time, was the busiest in the nation. Club member Cyrus Avery, a local insurance and real estate executive, used his position on the new federal highway commission to route one of the nation's first major highways, U.S. 66, through Tulsa.

Tulsa Country Club flourished along with the city. This is reflected in its continued evolution from a place for "loafing," as the early newspaper description put it, to a locus of Tulsa society. In this respect, it perhaps reached new heights as host of a reception for Gen. John J. Pershing on February 11, 1920. The World War I hero, with whom a number of Tulsans had served in the 1916 border campaign against Pancho Villa, had come to town to dedicate the hospital that is now Saint John Medical Center.

Downtown Tulsa, circa 1928. The Exchange National Bank Building—now the 320 S. Boston Building—are the tall buildings in the center.

But the club was quickly becoming a place where both men and women met for relaxation and sometimes for business. Later that year, *Tulsa World* society editor Lillian Crawford Perkins offered this useful, if somewhat convoluted, insight:

> [A] notable event in the early week was the dinner dance given in the country club by the officials and directors of the Union National Bank to stockholders and employees. In this was given, not only the opportunity for social mingling, which served a fine medium for binding closer the relationship needed between the bank's officials, the stockholders and employees, but in the after-dinner talks there was much said in a satisfying manner of the bank's history and its past and present success.

This growing popularity was in keeping with national trends. The number of U.S. country clubs quintupled from 1916 to 1923; and membership reached 2.7 million in 1927.

Postwar prosperity drove a great deal of this, but so did increasing acceptance of women's participation in outdoor sports—especially golf. Interest was such that Mehlhorn, while pro, instituted weekly nine-hole women's tournaments that drew as many as forty entrants. And when the state women's amateur came to town, it signaled a week of parties and social events covered by both the sports and society pages.

"Papers in the east," reported Perkins on October 24, 1920, "tell of club women taking up golf to get into condition for social activities for the winter."

Two prominent TCC women golfers during this period were two Ohio natives, Delight Bradstreet and Grace Ransom. Ransom organized and served as first president of the Women's Oklahoma Golf Association. She also belonged to the American Association of University Women and the "women's division" of Tulsa's Liberty Loan drives during World War II. Bradstreet, a dark, striking woman who shared a passion for the links with her husband, also presided over WOGA in its early years.

"With the suggestion that golfing and society may be correlated," wrote the society editor Perkins, "bring[s] a new thought and it is hoped that women in Tulsa remember that physical fortitude, as well

Clubhouse from Country Club Road, circa 1929.

as social pleasure, may be promoted by engaging in this most fascinating game."

The level of golf played during these years was remarkable. Although a rumored exhibition by British stars Harry Vardon and Ted Ray never materialized, other notables did make appearances. In 1921, Jim Kennedy and William Nichols lost 1-up in thirty-six holes to British Open champion Jock Hutchison and U.S. Open winner Jim Barnes at Muskogee. After Mehlhorn returned to Tulsa to win the 1923 Oklahoma Open, TCC hosted the event in 1925 and 1927. Ed Dudley, who went on to become Augusta National's first head pro, won the 1925 tournament. Among the 1927 entrants were Jock Hutchison and Gene Sarazen, who had already won a U.S. Open and two PGA Championships. They lost to Oklahoman Dick Grout, who years later, as a club pro in Columbus, Ohio, introduced a youngster named Jack Nicklaus to the game of golf.

Leadership, naturally, is important to any organization, and Tulsa Country Club during its early years was blessed with an abundance of it. Many of the city's leading citizens were members. Its presidents had included F. A. Leovy, an officer of Prairie Oil, and H. Y. "Cap" Arnold, a retired oilman and former Union Civil War officer who guided the club through the construction of the clubhouse following the 1915 fire. E. Rogers Kemp was a prominent businessman and one of the original incorporators. Dana Kelsey, who led the club through the years of the course redesign, had come to Oklahoma before statehood as a stenographer for the Indian Bureau and wound up a senior executive with Sinclair. Sam Kennedy, in effect the club's landlord, served two years as president in the mid-1920s.

Through those years, club presidents and directors faced their share of difficulties. None, however, would compare with the challenges looming in the decade ahead.

Ed Dudley was a little-known pro from Joplin, Missouri, when he won the 1925 Oklahoma Open at TCC. He later became the first head pro at Augusta National and president of the PGA.

Gene Sarazen had already won a U.S. Open and two PGA championships when he came to TCC for the 1927 Oklahoma Open. Besides Sarazen, the field included former British Open champion Jock Hutchison, but the winner was Dick Grout of Oklahoma City.

Downtown Tulsa as seen from the Osage Hills northwest of Tulsa Country Club around 1930. The Exchange National Bank Building and Philtower can be seen near the center of the photo. The Mayo Hotel and the spire of Holy Family Cathedral are on the right.

CHAPTER THREE

In the Rough

he 1930s began with great promise for Tulsa Country Club.

True, it was no longer the only club in town, much less the only golf course. Oakhurst Country Club—present-day Oaks—had opened in 1923. Indian Hills, east of Tulsa near Catoosa, opened a few years later, and the surrounding communities of Sand Springs, Sapulpa, Broken Arrow, and Skiatook all had country clubs. In addition, the city had built a course at Mohawk Park, and several privately owned public courses, including the Kennedy Golf Course adjoining TCC, were in operation.

This didn't seem to matter. Tulsa in those years carried itself with an air of invincibility and the optimism of youth. Two prosperous decades had built it into a city and transformed the club into something as close to an institution as could be found in a place so young and transient. The club operated on a comfortable cushion, enjoyed a large membership, and carried very little debt. The few telltale signs of impending economic catastrophe—falling industrial output, sinking commodity prices, even the October 1929 stock market collapse—were shrugged off as temporary interruptions of the seemingly endless good times.

In June the club was host to the Trans-Mississippi Golf Association women's championship. In an age when married women were almost never identified by their own first names and the term "female athlete" was regarded as an oxymoron, golf was one of the few women's sports with a wide following. And the Trans-Miss, while only four years old, was already one of the top women's tournaments in the country.

It drew nearly two hundred entries—a record—but no clear favorite. Opal Hill of Kansas City, the defending champion and 1929 U.S. Amateur winner, had been recruited by Glenna Collett Vare to play for the United States against England in a precursor to the Curtis Cup competition. Marion Turpin Lake, medalist in each of the three previous Trans-Miss tournaments, had left the area, as had 1927 champion and 1928 runner-up Miriam Burns Horn Tyson.

Attention soon turned to Dorothy Klotz Pardue of Sioux City, Iowa. The rangy Pardue, returning to competition after a two-year layoff, had turned down an invitation to Vare's Trans-Atlantic expedition. Her practice round at TCC "made a terrific impression," according to the June 2 *Tulsa World*, and soon she had galleries in excess of one thousand following her.

"She has a long, clean swing which approaches perfection in golfing form," the *World* reported as Pardue, battling first high winds and then rain, won medalist honors with an 83 and then marched through the match play brackets. In the quarterfinals, against four-time defending Oklahoma amateur champion Estelle Drennan of Tulsa, Pardue was two down after nine holes but rallied to win 3-and-1.

"Though she was sadly erratic with her woods and putter for nine holes, Mrs. Pardue brought gasps of admiration from the spectators with her power-

These early bylaws set annual dues at $36 with a $100 initiation fee.

ful drives," the *World* reported. "Despite the fact the soggy turf prevented any considerable roll, she was consistently about 220 yards from the tee with her first, to give her usually an advantage of 30 to 40 yards over her opponent."

In the final, Pardue met Mrs. Hulbert Clarke, a two-time state amateur champion from Oklahoma City. Deferential and self-deprecating, Clarke had systematically taken apart the other side of the bracket, beating Joyce Wallace of Sapulpa—soon to win the first of three state championships—5-and-4 in the semifinals. Although she was by this time a well-established golfer, Clarke's first name did not appear in any of the week's press reports or in the tournament records, and her last name was frequently misspelled.

But Clarke's steady irons and putter beat Pardue's big drives. On a rare June day, cool and windless, she won six straight holes early on and needed only thirty-one of the scheduled thirty-six holes to beat Pardue 6-and-5.

"Always outdriven and time after time a stroke behind as she came to the green, Mrs. Clarke would make up the deficit and frequently win the hole in the last hundred yards," reported *World* sports editor B. A. Bridgewater.

"I don't see how it happened," the surprised winner said. "She's four times a better player than I am. She was just off, that's all."

By September 1931, even Tulsa was feeling the pinch. Added to the deepening worldwide depression, the opening of the East Texas field had sent oil prices into a free fall that would eventually lead Gov. William H. Murray to send the National Guard to shut down Oklahoma production until prices rebounded.

One of the nation's greatest natural disasters of all time, a drought soon to become known as the Dust Bowl, had already taken hold. Will Rogers appeared in Tulsa on a charity relief tour, and the local community fund set an unprecedented goal of $250,000, a figure that soon proved wholly inadequate.

For some, golf—and life—continued more or less as before. Two young Tulsa Country Club stars, Jack Malloy and Sam Kennedy Jr., distinguished themselves that August at Broadmoor. But, in what may have been a warning of things to come, the Oklahoma Open at Tulsa Country Club drew fewer than seventy entries instead of the expected one hundred.

Held for the first time separately from the state amateur, the tournament consisted of an eighteen-hole pro-am warm-up and seventy-two holes of medal play packed into one weekend. Favorites included state amateur champ Henry Robertson, a product of former TCC pro Art Jackson's program at Lincoln Park in Oklahoma City, and Oklahoma PGA champion Bob Higgins of Okmulgee. The leading out-of-state entry was Harold "Jug" McSpaden, a twenty-three-year-old Kansas City pro destined for PGA stardom. A newcomer, Oklahoma City Twin Hills pro Floyd Farley, attracted attention by shooting a 71 for his practice round. Local entrants included TCC's George Johnston and Logan Van Zandt.

Low scores were expected after four best-ball teams finished the pro-am at 4-under-par, but the field returned to the course the next morning to find the pins devilishly repositioned. And it was windy. Wrote Bridgewater:

> The big rolling greens . . . on which the cups can be tucked away in the most exasperating spots, and a brisk south wind [that] carried the large ball where it wasn't meant to

go, aided the natural defenses of the layout in turning back the onslaughts of the 67 entrants who unsuccessfully attacked Old Man Par.

"Large ball" referred to the new dimensions set earlier that year by the U.S. Golf Association: 1.68 inches minimum diameter and 1.55 ounces maximum weight. This was a slightly larger, lighter ball than previously in use. In 1932, the weight limit was raised to 1.62 ounces, and the "large ball" became, despite British resistance, the worldwide standard still in use today.

Not a single golfer broke par during the first two rounds of the 1931 Oklahoma Open, and the leader at the halfway point was John Winters, a Tulsa stockbroker and TCC member with a very modest golfing resume. Winters, who would later become president of the U.S. Golf Association, thrashed his way to a 5-over 74-73—147 and a two-stroke lead on Van Zandt and McSpaden. Oakhurst pro Jack Guild and Oscar Bowman, the TCC greenskeeper, were three back.

"One man after another three- and four-putted away his chances," wrote Bridgewater. "It was estimated that placing the cups in difficult places on the greens made the course fully eight strokes more difficult than the normal 71."

Dick Grout, who had won the same tournament on the same course just four years earlier, took twenty-nine strokes on just two holes—two and eighteen—for the two rounds and was still in contention. Johnston was ten shots back and Higgins twelve.

McSpaden, who had been "all over the course" through the first two rounds, was the favorite going into the second day. For a while, it looked as if that was indeed how the tournament would go. Winters continued to play steadily in the morning round, shooting another 73, but McSpaden beat par with a 70 to take a one-shot lead.

Fatigue took hold in the afternoon, however. McSpaden began spraying the ball around again and took a 42 on the front nine. Winters began "dubbing" approach shots and soared to an 85. Guild couldn't putt. Van Zandt kept getting lost off the tee and wound up disqualifying himself because of a scorecard error. Meanwhile, back at the clubhouse, Oklahoma City amateur E. J. Rogers watched with growing excitement as his final-round 72 and 298 total remained at the top of the leaderboard.

Rogers had been on the fringes of the lead throughout the tournament but appeared out of contention when his 75 for the second day's morning round put him seven shots behind McSpaden. And, at the end, it looked like McSpaden might win after all. Righting himself on the back nine, the Kansas City pro shot a 34 and birdied two of the last four holes. He still came up one stroke short.

Rogers thus became the first amateur to win the Oklahoma Open. He would go on to win state amateur titles in 1932 and 1940.

Tulsa Country Club, which had hosted seven of the first twenty-two Opens, would not see another for seventeen years.

The 1931 Oklahoma Open was significant for at least one other reason: the Tulsa debut of Walter Emery.

Emery was then a University of Tulsa student and belonged to Indian Hills Country Club. He joined Tulsa Country Club sometime before World War II but didn't settle in Tulsa permanently until the late 1940s. But even as a teenager, Walter Emery cut an instantly recognizable figure.

"Emery [is] a slim youth who plays amazingly good golf except on the grass greens, which are new

Clubhouse for James Kennedy's public course opened during the 1920s. Torn down in the 1960s, it stood near the site of the present TCC clubhouse.

The starter shed for the Kennedy Golf Course was near the present first green.

A prominent figure in Oklahoma golf for four decades, Walter Emery made a favorable impression with his performance in the 1931 Oklahoma Open at Tulsa Country Club. Emery was the first player from west of the Mississippi River to win an NCAA golf title.

to him," Bridgewater wrote after the first day of the 1931 Open.

Emery finished well down the list that year, but his best golf lay ahead. More than that, he became one of Oklahoma golf's most colorful characters, a fixture on the fairways and in the clubhouse for four decades and then some.

"Even when he was a 'serious' golfer," the *Tulsa Tribune*'s Bob Hartzell wrote in 1973, "Emery wasn't too serious about anything."

He was born in Nowata but grew up all over the world as his father, S. W. Emery, followed the scent of one oil field after another. Walter finished high school at Duncan, where he won the state high school championship in 1931. He enrolled at TU, and then transferred to the University of Oklahoma, where he became the first player from west of the Mississippi River to win the NCAA title. In 1935, he was runner-up to Lawson Little in the U.S. Amateur and won the Oklahoma Open. The following year, he won the state amateur and played on the U.S. Walker Cup team. Emery also won the 1939 state amateur and played in the first Masters. Some observers considered him Oklahoma's best golfer of all time up through the 1960s. Emery probably could have won some money on the pro circuit, but his father talked him out of it.

"He said the way I putted, I would always be a triple-A player, and there was no room in golf for a triple-A player," Emery told Hartzell.

Instead, Emery got a law degree from OU, served in the Navy during World War II, and eventually went into the insurance business in Tulsa. High-level competitive golf was behind him by then, but his trademark safari helmet remained a common sight on Oklahoma courses, and especially at TCC, until shortly before his death in 1980.

Emery was at least as much an attraction in the grillroom as he was on the tee box. There, over drinks and a cheeseburger, he regaled with tales of exploits on and off the links. A favorite was his description of arriving at Pine Valley, New Jersey, for the 1936 Walker Cup competition in a coal truck. This is the version he told Hartzell:

> "They gave me $9.50 for taxi fare from Philadelphia to Pine Valley. They knew what they were doing but I didn't. There was a Pine Valley train stop and the fare was only 35 cents from Philadelphia to there. That $9.50 was a lot of money in those days, so I thought I would save some of it.
>
> "But the Pine Valley train stop was only a little shed, a combination grocery store and bar, and a combination coal and ice plant. The lady at the grocery store said there were no taxis but that the guy who drove the coal and ice truck would be back pretty soon and might take me to the club.
>
> "So I spent part of my $9 in the bar waiting for him and the rest of it after he got there. Then we climbed into that old Chevy truck and it didn't have brake one. . . . There was a big hill going down to the clubhouse . . . . We came roaring down that hill and the ol' boy slapped it into second and then into low.
>
> "Then this guy from the country club comes out in his red blazer and says, 'Service entrance to the rear.'"

In a sanitized version of the story, Emery replied: "To heck with you, you son-of-a-gun, I'm playing in this dad-blamed tournament."

By the end of 1933, unemployed men lucky enough to get jobs with the Civil Works Administration were walking as far as seven miles in freezing temperatures to work on a construction crew at Mohawk Park for $2.40 a day. Sheriff sales for Tulsa County that year topped $3.1 million. The Community Fund, forerunner of the United Way, had declared itself insolvent halfway through 1932; the county, which bore governmental responsibility for poverty relief in the absence of any state or federal agency, said it had no more money, either. Starving people were given packets of seeds to plant in donated garden plots.

By the second half of 1934, things were beginning to look a bit brighter. More than eleven thousand Tulsa County families were on relief, but other economic indicators, including bank deposits, building permits, and retail trade, had improved. Golf had persevered and in at least one ironic way prospered—the CWA project at Mohawk Park included improvements to the golf course.

The Depression's effect on Tulsa Country Club is difficult to judge from this distance. In 1933, it paid off the last of $100,000 in bonds issued ten years before and declared itself debt-free. In the 1933 annual report, presented at a stockholders banquet on January 15, 1934, club president Frank Rodolf insisted the worst was over.

> Your Directors are happy to report that the Tulsa Country Club weathered the recent stormy months in excellent fashion. The club has remained out of debt and has continued on a cash basis without lessening service or discontinuing any department. The year 1933 proved better in every respect than that of 1932.

The club even reported an operating profit of about $6,000. According to club lore, at least some of that was owed to the popularity of slot machines clattering away more or less openly in the clubhouse. If so, Tulsa Country Club would not have been alone.

Slot machines and other forms of gambling were among the many devices employed by country clubs in the struggle to remain solvent during the Depression. From 1927 to 1934, American country clubs lost nearly 80 percent of their members. Most clubs survived but were forced to make changes. They installed swimming pools and built riding stables to appeal to non-golfers. Children were more in evidence.

"In the 1930s," writes James M. Mayo in his book *The American Country Club: Its Origins and Development*, "country clubs became family oriented out of economic necessity."

An unsigned typescript in the club archives attests to a similar transformation for Tulsa Country

Club: "The swimming pool was built [in 1935] and this was the beginning of real use of the club by families of members. Here-to-fore very few people used the club except Golfers and meals were only served on reservations made several days in advance."

For Don Eustice, the club was practically his backyard. As a boy, he lived across the street from the little house on the south side of the course where club pro Joe Dahlman and his family made their home. Eustice and Dahlman's son Richard spent many happy days on the course.

"When we were about seven, we'd come over and knock balls around on the course," Eustice recalled in a 2007 interview. "It was like home to me. We'd fish in the ponds on the golf course. Nobody cared as long as we stayed out of the way."

Later, the Eustice family moved to the 1100 block of North Elwood, just east of the club.

"There wasn't anything there," Eustice said, "just blank ground between our house and the course. We mowed us out a little place and set up our own course."

Perhaps more pressing than the economic times were the demands of some of TCC's own members and the community at large. While the club's directors steered a conservative and what seemed to them prudent course through the financial straits of the time, others apparently favored a more aggressive tack. Rodolf's somewhat defensive remarks in the 1933 annual report hint at the intramural tension.

> It has seemed the part of wisdom to retain the present low-rent lease until the most trying part of the depression passed, and we believe time has proved the soundness of the idea. We are happy to report that recent conferences with Dr. Kennedy and his family permit us to announce that before the next annual meeting, we will have extended our lease on a term which is eminently fair to the club and a signal evidence of the generosity of Dr. Kennedy and his family. In this connection, let it be again stated that Dr. Kennedy has always been most fair; his attitude has ever been paternal and sincere [with] the interests of the club being the foremost consideration.

Don Eustice first played at Tulsa Country Club in the 1930s. Growing up across the street from the club in the 1930s—in a house that still stands—his association with TCC spans more than seventy years.

Beneath the surface, pressure mounted for the club to expand or move. TCC had for a number of years had a reciprocal agreement with the Tulsa Club, a downtown citadel of the city's elite. About 60 percent of TCC's membership belonged to both organizations, and for several years the two had talked intermittently about merging. In October 1934, the *Tulsa Tribune* reported negotiations were on again.

These discussions seem to have included a buyout of the Kennedy property and enough additional acreage for a second course. At the same time, oilman Waite Phillips was approached about a three-hundred-acre farm he owned southeast of town. He agreed to donate the land. According to a January 6, 1935, report in the *Tulsa World*, golf course architect Perry Maxwell had been "looking over the site for a year or more."

A four-man committee handling negotiations between the clubs said just before Christmas that members would be asked to vote on a merger. If the merger were approved, members would then be asked whether they wanted to expand the existing Tulsa Country Club to thirty-six holes on land leased from the Kennedy family, or build a new club on the Phillips acreage. For reasons not fully explained, the vote never took place.

Instead, it was announced on January 2, 1935, that a new organization separate from both Tulsa Country Club and the Tulsa Club had been formed to build Southern Hills Country Club on the Phillips property. Half the two hundred founding memberships, at $1,000 each, were pledged the first night. The rest were soon sold, too.

Later written accounts attributed the breakdown of negotiations between TCC and the Tulsa Club to S. G. Kennedy's unwillingness to renew the lease due to expire at the end of 1935, or on his supposed demand that the club buy the leased site for an exorbitant price. If so, no contemporary report to that effect can be found; Rodolf's remarks in the 1933 annual report, in fact, indicate just the opposite. Kennedy himself was known for proclaiming, "I only buy, never sell" when it came to real estate.

Other accounts state the so-called Tulsa Club faction believed the Kennedys wanted to take the TCC course public. Again, the contemporary reports suggest something a little different.

If the Kennedys had ever been reluctant to renew the TCC lease, they were not by the end of 1934. Indeed, they offered to extend it for up to twenty years and to include the public Kennedy Golf Course in the deal. What seems more likely is that the Tulsa Club faction was unwilling to invest the money needed for the changes it wanted on property it did not own. The Kennedys, in turn, probably either refused to sell or set a price deemed unacceptable by the Tulsa Club faction—especially in light of Phillips's offer to donate the Southern Hills property.

The Southern Hills announcement brought predictions of dire consequences for Tulsa Country Club. True, it was more financially secure than the other clubs in the area, but it also had more at stake. Many TCC members and even some of its officers were part of the Southern Hills venture. On January 12, Tulsa Country Club President Frank Rodolf issued a statement congratulating Southern Hills and declaring it a sign of confidence in the city's continued growth.

"While welcoming the new club we ask our members to retain faith in the progress and continuance of the Tulsa Country Club," Rodolf wrote. "It is inconceivable that the Southern Hills will be the last course constructed for Tulsa."

TCC did have some advantages. It was still more convenient for most members than Southern Hills, and its strong financial position allowed it to build a $15,000 swimming pool and make other improvements without going into debt. And, it was cheaper. While Southern Hills' equity memberships were sold for $1,000, TCC's were about $300 with monthly dues of eleven dollars.

The Kennedy lease was indeed extended in 1935, this time through 1950, but the mid-1930s could not have been easy. Memberships sold for as little as one hundred dollars. In November 1936, the *Tribune* reported that Dahlman, the club pro since 1927, was being replaced. It wasn't that Dahlman hadn't done a good job. He had. But he was not much of a tournament golfer, and it was thought bringing in someone new might "stimulate interest and stir up renewed activity."

Yet, just a few days earlier, the *World* reported a net membership increase of thirty-three over the previous year. True, 153 members had been lost, but 186 new ones had been added, bringing the total to 344 with 375 expected by the end of the year.

The corner, it seemed, had been turned.

The present No. 6 has become a signature hole for Tulsa Country Club. The old stone bridge in the background is thought to date from the 1930s.

Patti Blanton won the last of her four Oklahoma women's amateur titles at Tulsa Country Club in 1948. Blanton also won two state amateurs in both Colorado and Kansas and the 1952 Trans-Miss.

CHAPTER FOUR

War and Peace

The color was coming back to the cheeks of Tulsa's economy in December 1941. Bank deposits were up. So were retail sales and employment. But all was not well, for over this growing prosperity gathered darkening clouds.

In 1940, the War Department approved a $23 million bomber factory to be built adjacent to the Tulsa airport. Ordnance works were built near Chouteau and Baxter Springs, Kansas. Reserves and National Guardsmen were activated and trained for combat. European refugees began arriving in Tulsa. And every day, the news from Europe and the Far East seemed to be worse.

On December 3, 1941, the *Tulsa World*'s front page carried the ominous headline "Zero Hour Is Near" over a story foretelling crisis in the Pacific. Four days later, on December 7, early morning readers encountered an editorial declaring, "the United States is right up against a stern situation and all of us are in it."

Within hours, Tulsa and the rest of America would know the situation was stern indeed.

All problems paled in comparison to that day's attack on Pearl Harbor and the sobering reality of war. Telegrams began to arrive, informing parents of dead and wounded sons. Panic gripped the West Coast, and even Tulsa made preparations for air raids. The economy moved quickly to wartime footing, with consumer goods ranging from foodstuffs to automobiles becoming scarce or nonexistent almost overnight.

And yet, as a practical matter, country clubs had to find a way to survive.

The clubs were still recovering from the Depression when the bombs fell on Pearl Harbor. They may have become more "family friendly," but golf remained their financial life's blood, and the number of active golfers in the United States had declined by 20 percent in ten years. Now a substantial number of club members—not to mention club pros, groundskeepers, and other employees—were going into the military while those left behind were exhorted to spend whatever spare money they had on war bonds.

Many Americans, historian John Strege writes in his 2005 book *When War Played Through*, felt it inappropriate to play golf while others died on foreign battlefields. Those who did play had difficulty finding equipment. Within days of Pearl Harbor, the federal government ordered an 80 percent reduction in nonmilitary use of rubber, effectively ending the manufacture of golf balls.

In January 1942, the U.S. Golf Association cancelled all of its national championships for the war's duration. Sam Snead enlisted in the Navy the day after winning the 1942 PGA. Ben Hogan gave up golf and moved briefly to Tulsa for flight training at Spartan School of Aeronautics before entering the Army Air Corps. Bobby Jones, at age forty, successfully appealed his 4-F classification and was inducted into the Army Air Corps while cattle grazed the fairways of his beloved Augusta National Golf Club, shuttered because of wartime travel restrictions. Winners of the few professional tournaments still played were often paid in war bonds rather than cash. Closer to home, the Tulsa District Golf Association ceased operation, and the Oklahoma Golf Association cancelled its state tournaments beginning in 1943.

Club golf continued, however. It had been given something of a boost early in the war when the government endorsed the game as a suitable activity for maintaining civilian physical fitness. Later, golf would be employed as therapy for injured soldiers, some of whom learned the game under the tutelage of Hogan himself.

The effect of the war on Tulsa Country Club can be partly judged from surviving club records. Many memberships were suspended because of military service. Members of the staff were drafted or enlisted and sometimes didn't return. "We are informed that former caddy master John Mahoney has been killed in the line of duty," notes the board minutes of January 18, 1944.

On February 15, the board authorized the purchase of $8,000 in war bonds. On March 9, it voted to pay club manager A. Danner Grimes fifty dollars a month during his military service.

The club seems to have been profitable despite the difficulties of the time. With gas rationed and tires and auto parts scarce, it probably benefited to at least some extent by its proximity to downtown. The club also benefited, on balance, by a political quirk that placed it outside both the city limits and Tulsa County.

In the run up to statehood, the Osage Indians had insisted their former reservation be preserved as a single entity. This provision created uncertainty as to whether the City of Tulsa could annex adjoining portions of Osage County. Or, perhaps more

Ben Hogan was among the golf stars who left the pro tour for military service during World War II. He briefly lived in Tulsa while training at Spartan School of Aeronautics, returning in 1946 to finish second in the one and only Southwestern Invitational at Southern Hills.

precisely, it provided Tulsa cover for not extending its boundaries into Osage County. Oklahoma's creaky municipal finance laws made annexation a losing proposition; this was especially true for Tulsa, which, until the advent of the city sales tax in the 1960s, derived most of its operating revenues from selling water at retail rates to customers outside the city limits.

In any event, the circumstances left Tulsa Country Club in the unusual position of setting perhaps a mile from Tulsa City Hall and the Tulsa County Courthouse but outside the jurisdiction of both. Thus, the clandestine slot machines kept whirling, and bootleggers kept making deliveries. The extent to which the club feared enforcement of the liquor laws is perhaps best reflected in the expenditure of $60,000 in 1940 to renovate the cocktail lounge—and this in a state in which liquor of any kind was supposed to be illegal. Surely the admonition to the club manager, recorded in the board minutes every January for years, to "rigidly enforce all rules and regulations in regard to gambling and drinking on club premises," must have been delivered with the heaviest of irony.

As for golf, the biggest problem seems to have been finding enough serviceable balls. The day after restrictions on civilian use of rubber were announced in December 1941, Abercrombie & Fitch, then one of the nation's leading suppliers of golf balls, sold twenty-four thousand in two hours at its New York store. Spalding Dots, considered the best ball then made, were scarfed up by the hundred dozen, so that by the end of 1942 they were practically worth their weight in gold.

Most ball coverings of the era were balata, a sappy substance similar to gutta percha that cut easily. But golfers had to make do. Even tour professionals were reduced to hoarding and playing with recycled balls. Sam Snead claimed to have played fifty-four holes of one event with a single soft, lopsided ball.

Some clubs hired divers to retrieve balls from water hazards or drained the ponds altogether to get them.

Charity exhibitions for the benefit of the Red Cross and other war-related causes proliferated. Entertainers Bob Hope and Bing Crosby were frequent headliners, as were tour pros Byron Nelson and Harold "Jug" McSpaden, both of whom had been declared physically unfit for military service. Between them, the Gold Dust Twins as they were known, dominated wartime golf.

In September 1944, Nelson and McSpaden stopped in Tulsa for an exhibition hastily arranged by Tulsa Country Club Green Committee chairman Lee Murdock, among others. Nelson and McSpaden were originally to play against local club pros Bill Wotherspoon and George Whitehead, but Ky Laffoon, a former Tulsan then playing out of Chicago, threw down an undoubtedly scripted challenge that sounded like something out of the professional wrestling circuit of the day. Instead of Wotherspoon and Whitehead—both more than respectable golfers—the Gold Dust Twins went up against Laffoon and George Schneiter, a nifty putter probably best remembered as the PGA's first tournament supervisor.

A word here about Ky Laffoon. Born in Zinc, Arkansas, and raised among the mines of extreme northeastern Oklahoma, Laffoon was reputed to have become head professional of what is now Miami, Oklahoma, Country Club at age fifteen. Early in Laffoon's tour career, a Chicago writer incorrectly identified him as part Indian; Laffoon liked the idea so much he created an entirely fictional Cherokee ancestry for himself. Occasionally brilliant but more often erratic, Laffoon could be murder on clubs that didn't hit the ball where he wanted. According to one story, after a particularly unfortunate case of the yips, Laffoon walked straight from the eighteenth green to the parking lot, retrieved a revolver from the trunk of his car, and shot his putter three times. "That'll teach ya," he is supposed to have said.

No gunplay was reported the day Laffoon and the others toured Tulsa Country Club, but the event nonetheless produced its share of excitement. More than three thousand fans paid $1.25 each for a thirty-minute mini-clinic by McSpaden and Nelson and to watch Schneiter steal the show with a 68 that included a twenty-five-foot birdie putt on No. 3. McSpaden shot 70, Nelson 71, and Laffoon 74. Although he hadn't much to do with it, Laffoon made good on his dare as he and Schneiter beat McSpaden and Nelson 2-and-1.

"Pros at the various country clubs and public courses should get set for their banner weekend of the season," wrote B. A. Bridgewater. "Hundreds in that crowd at the country club who thought they had given up golf for the duration will certainly feel the urge to play again after watching the crack pros assault par."

Unlike many clubs and public courses, TCC apparently managed to marshal enough resources

Kansas City pro Harold "Jug" McSpaden appeared often at Tulsa Country Club during the 1930s and 1940s. He narrowly lost the 1931 Oklahoma Open at TCC to Emmett Rogers and played two exhibitions at the club with his friend Byron Nelson during World War II. Declared physically unfit for military service, the two became known as the "Gold Dust Twins" for their domination of wartime golf.

George Schneiter bested Byron Nelson, Jug McSpaden, and Ky Laffoon in a 1944 exhibition at Tulsa Country Club. Schneiter later became the PGA's first tournament supervisor.

"Lee Murdock, Jimmy Duck, Morgan Jones, Bob Collins and some of the other boys who took a leading part in bringing Nelson and McSpaden here for the exhibition were glowing, and had a right to," wrote Bridgewater.

The exhibition originally was to have been for charity, but a sponsorship fell through and instead the proceeds became seed money for a proposed PGA Tour stop. The Southwestern Invitational—called the Tulsa Open in some references—made its one and only appearance on the PGA schedule in September 1945. Sam Snead, fresh off a victory in Dallas, scorched Southern Hills for a 72-hole 277 and one of his record eighty-two official career victories.

Four months before winning at Southern Hills, though, Snead finished a shot behind Nelson in a charity exhibition at Tulsa Country Club.

The match was played on May 8, 1945, under nearly ideal conditions and with Tulsa and the rest of the nation alive with the news of Adolf Hitler's death and the surrender of Germany. Organized

NELSON 68, SNEAD 69 AT TCC

to keep its links in fine shape through the war.

"The TCC greens always did excite our admiration," Bridgewater said, "and they've rarely been in better shape than they are right now."

Nelson, who had won a tournament in Dallas two days earlier, may have been a little fatigued. Still, he drew gasps from the crowd on No. 15 when, as the *World*'s John Turner put it, he "came up with a bit of the brilliance that has earned him the name Mr. Golf of 1944."

Nelson's tee shot flew down the middle. He pitched his second to within three feet of the pin and finished off the hole with a birdie putt.

Byron Nelson and Sam Snead squared off on May 8, 1945, shortly after Snead's discharge from the Navy.

A gallery watches Byron Nelson with the TCC clubhouse in the background. Nelson played two exhibitions at the club during World War II. The first featured Nelson, Jug McSpaden, Ky Laffoon, and George Schneiter. This photo was probably taken during Nelson's second visit in 1945.

by the sports committee of the local Chamber of Commerce, the event raised money for a nine-hole rehabilitation golf course at a military hospital in Chickasha.

Snead's appearance attracted attention throughout the state. His return to the tour after his discharge from the Navy the previous winter had sparked renewed interest in the game. It also meant the end of Nelson's unquestioned dominance.

"There is real rivalry between Nelson and Snead—and all the golfers know it," wrote Bridgewater.

Bridgewater predicted both would shoot in the 60s.

"It couldn't exactly be said Nelson and McSpaden lacked for inspiration in their last Tulsa visit," Bridgewater explained. "George Schneiter was shooting well enough to hold anybody's attention. . . . But Nelson and McSpaden were not ruffled by this performance . . . . They were glad to see Schneiter do well. They feel differently about Snead. They'll be after him every step of the way."

McSpaden, as usual, played with Nelson. Snead's teammate had been chosen through a tournament that attracted most of the area's top amateurs and club professionals, including Jimmy Nichols, the one-armed pro at McAlester Country Club. The winner, though, was Buck Gann, a strapping 225-pound Tulsa firefighter who sank a twenty-foot putt on the last hole of regulation to force an eighteen-hole playoff with Ivy Leaguer Dick Pringle. Gann won the playoff by seven strokes.

Nelson and McSpaden won 3-and-2, but it hardly mattered. The 2,500 on hand were there to see some shots, and they were not disappointed.

Tulsa firefighter Buck Gann earned the right to play with Byron Nelson, Ben Hogan, and Jug McSpaden at Tulsa Country Club by winning a tournament that attracted some of the best golfers in the region. Gann, a strapping six feet four inches, shot a respectable 78 on his big day.

Sam Snead shot a 69, one more than Byron Nelson, in a match-play exhibition in May 1945. The event also featured Jug McSpaden and a local fireman named Buck Gann. Later that same year, Snead won the Southwestern Invitational at Southern Hills by nine shots over Ben Hogan.

"Lord Byron Nelson, professional master of the irons, put on a superb exhibition," wrote the *World*'s John Turner.

"Slammin' Sam, who lived up to his reputation as a terrific driver . . . also stole the putting show from McSpaden by curling in a 40-footer on No. 5 and a 30-footer on No. 10."

Nelson shot 68, Snead 69. McSpaden, as was often his wont, provided some thrills but ultimately suffered from a few too many adventures into woods and water and finished with a 73. Gann, his howitzer-like drives drawing gasps from the crowd, gamely batted out a 78.

Nelson left the tour only two years later. He never lost his competitiveness, though, at least not when it came to Snead. Many years after their TCC exhibition, Nelson returned for a dinner. Barely able to walk, he was led into the club's trophy room where framed photos of him, Snead, and McSpaden hang. Turning to Jim Unruh, a longtime club member and USGA official, Nelson said curtly, "Unruh, I've got a problem."

"What's that?"

Pointing to Snead's picture, Nelson said, "My friend's picture is signed. Mine isn't. You think we could do something about that?"

The request did not have to be made twice. Quickly, Nelson's photo was taken down from the wall and removed from its frame so he could autograph it.

The 1940s marked a transitional period in the leadership of Tulsa Country Club. The founders and early members were fast fading from the scene. In 1937, the club had elected Ed Leroux president. A recent arrival from Muskogee, Leroux would remain in office for more than a decade, until his death in 1947. Regular turnover in club management ended in 1940 when Danner Grimes and Earl Kauffman were hired; Grimes remained general manager until 1952, except for a two-year hitch in the Navy when Kauffman ran the club, and Kauffman took over when Grimes left to open his own restaurant. Also worth noting was the retirement of headwaiter Phil Goolsby after nearly thirty years with club; the board voted Goolsby a half-salary pension of $37.50 per month for life.

The most noteworthy change, though, was the death on September 27, 1941, of Dr. Samuel Grant

Kennedy. For Tulsa and Tulsa Country Club, it was like losing a father.

Kennedy and his brother James had come to Tulsa in 1891, when the town was just a muddy little stop on the St. Louis and San Francisco Railway. They were Tulsa's first real doctors; their office was Tulsa's first brick building. Years later, when a developer pulled out of an unfinished office building at Fourth Street and Boston Avenue, Kennedy took over the project and expanded it into the landmark that still bears his name. An adventurous soul, he had participated in three land runs and homesteaded in the no man's land that became the Oklahoma Panhandle. At his funeral, a broke wagon wheel paid silent homage to his early role in the community.

But, like most patriarchs, Kennedy left an ambiguous legacy. Kennedy was among the early Tulsans who had believed the city's primary growth would be northward, along the spine of Denver Avenue toward the bluff that became known as Reservoir Hill. It is not unreasonable to think he envisioned TCC as a spur for that growth.

Instead, Tulsa spread south and east, and Kennedy felt betrayed by the city's refusal to annex the southeast corner of Osage County or help in its development. By the terms of the trust he left behind, Kennedy forbid the development of his land—nearly ten square miles—until twenty years after his death. To the north and west, the area around Tulsa Country Club would remain open prairie until the 1960s.

A little girl lived upstairs in the sprawling mansion of a clubhouse on Country Club Road. Her name was Danna Sue, after her father Danner Grimes, the club manager, and from the time she was born until she started the sixth grade, Tulsa Country Club was quite literally her home.

"I had great slumber parties," she remembers. "After the members were gone and nobody was there, we had the place to ourselves. We would go into the cocktail lounge and put cherries and limes and all those toppings in our Cokes. Everybody wanted to come to my house."

The Grimes family lived in an apartment on the top floor of the clubhouse. Danna Sue—now Danna Sue Walker—remembers it as spacious but oddly laid out.

"Our apartment had a very strange entrance. You either went around to the back and came up some stairs, or you had to go through the lady's powder room to get to our front door," she said.

Danna Sue Walker, longtime society editor of the Tulsa World, *spent her first dozen years living upstairs in the TCC clubhouse while her father, Danner Grimes, managed the club.*

"I'd go down the stairs, and there would be that huge, huge formal part, looking out on the pool and golf course. Downstairs was the grill and the women's locker room. Daddy had slot machines for a while, and the slot machines were in the sitting room in the women's locker room. I remember sneaking in and putting nickels in them when I was in grade school."

There were some disadvantages. It took the longest time for Danna Sue to convince her parents to let her have a dog. And on the rare occasions she was allowed to camp out, she had to be back inside before daylight.

But the staff was like an extended family; once, when a pet bird died, the headwaiter organized a funeral complete with appropriate music.

The little girl moved out in 1952, when Danner Grimes opened a cafeteria in newly built Utica Square. But she never forgot what it was like living in the big house on the hill.

"I remember thinking how elegant it was, and what a fun, fun place it was to live," she recalls. "I was this only child [who] had the whole club as playground.

"I still have dreams about it."

The Tam O'Shanter All-American, a sort of unofficial U.S. Open held in Chicago during the war years, attracted 105,000 spectators in the summer of 1945. A Hope-Crosby exhibition at the same course drew 25,000. PGA President Ed Dudley, the one-time Joplin pro who had won the 1925 Oklahoma Open at Tulsa Country Club and gone on to become the first head professional at Augusta National, confidently predicted "the greatest [golf] boom of all time."

Japan's surrender on August 14 lit the fuse. Celebrations had been restrained after Germany's capitulation three months earlier, but now Tulsa went wild along with the rest of the country. President Harry Truman declared a two-day national holiday. In downtown Tulsa, office workers dumped wastebaskets full of paper out of upper story windows and servicemen walked around looking for girls to kiss.

Six weeks later, eleven thousand watched Sam Snead win the Southwestern Invitational at Southern Hills by nine shots over "diminutive Benny Hogan" and former PGA champ Vic Ghezzi, with Byron Nelson a distant fourth. After more than a decade in the doldrums, golf was indeed on its way back.

For Tulsa Country Club, the evidence was a sharp increase in demand for memberships. The number of shareholding members had already been raised from 420 to 450 in March 1944, and a year later the membership rolls were closed altogether, creating the first waiting list in a long time if not ever.

By April 1946, the cost of memberships had increased from $100 during the war to $400. In October, the price went to $600.

In January of that year, the club had hired gentlemanly Morrie Gravatt as head pro. A native of Florida who began caddying at age eight and turned pro at sixteen, Gravatt had finished in the money in twenty-two straight tour events in 1945, no mean accomplishment. He remained TCC head pro until 1955, when a bad back convinced him to give up golf for private business.

"He was a very nice man and a very good golfer," recalled Jim Unruh.

But he apparently didn't much care for plus fours, the old-style golf trousers so named for being four inches longer than regular knickers. Unruh explained:

I think it was 1947 or '48. Southern Hills had its first member-guest tournament after the war. The guy my grandfather was working for brought some guy nobody had ever heard of. His name was Haggar. He was *that* Haggar. He was just really getting his slacks business going. He said, "Come out to the car with me." He opened up his trunk and gave my friend and me some slacks, bright green and canary yellow. And here were these plus fours. And we wore them.

But not at TCC. Before Unruh could venture onto the course in them, Gravatt told him, "Don't show up in plus fours."

"I don't think he liked those bright-colored slacks, either," said Unruh.

World War II's end caused a brief hiccup in Tulsa's economy, brought on by the closing of the Douglas bomber plant and the cessation of other defense industries. City leaders were prepared for this inevitable eventuality, however, and in January 1946, a city-owned public trust acquired the Douglas facility and leased it to American Airlines. American, in turn, announced it was moving its primary maintenance operations as well as its accounting center and stewardess training—the title "flight attendant" had not yet been invented—to Tulsa.

Nothing since the Ida Glenn No. 1 erupted over the top of the derrick changed Tulsa's future and direction more than the coming of American Airlines. Tulsa knew it could not be the Oil Capital forever; the arrival of American and the related industries that followed preserved and expanded an economic base temporarily broadened by wartime manufacturing, and created for Tulsa a new identity. Oklahoma jobs grew by forty-nine thousand in April

1948 and fifty-nine thousand in May. In the first week of June, unemployment dipped to 1 percent in Tulsa as the number of people working climbed 73 percent in fifteen months.

That same week, Tulsa Country Club played host to its first major statewide event in a decade, the state women's amateur. Leading the record field of 126 entrants was former Tulsan Patti Blanton, winner of three Oklahoma and five Kansas state championships. Two other former champions, TCC member Joyce Wallace and Oklahoma City's Jenny Grout, were also entered.

The TCC course was rated a par 71 for men but 78 for women, with four devilish par 3s "that call for exacting golf," in the words of the *World*'s John Turner. The most vexing of these, Turner said, was No. 14, "a small elevated green that is an easy deuce or a hard 10."

On the same day that Citation won the Belmont Stakes and racing's Triple Crown, Blanton won her fourth and last Oklahoma state title, beating Margaret Boardman of Tulsa 6-and-4 in the thirty-six-hole championship. The match was notable for the two finalists' strength and finesse. Boardman had hit the ball nearly three hundred yards to win the tournament long-drive contest. Blanton matched her for length once the title was on the line and putted almost flawlessly.

In September, the Oklahoma Open returned to TCC for the first time since 1931. The thirty-six-hole tournament attracted 104 entries, more than half of them professionals. Jimmy Gauntt, head pro at Oklahoma City's Twin Hills Country Club, shot a two-under 140 to win by two strokes over Ted Gwin, a former TCC member who had given up an accounting job with Douglas to become assistant pro at Southern Hills.

In mid-1949, Tulsa Country Club listed 568 total members. The course was in good shape. The clubhouse was bursting at the seams.

"The country clubs that survived the Great Depression and World War II were financially hardened," writes historian James Mayo. "The country club was treated as a business."

And business was good.

Among the best of the young female golfers to come along in the 1950s, TCC's Betsy Cullen won two state junior titles and three state amateurs before turning pro in the 1960s. She spent fourteen years on the LPGA tour.

CHAPTER FIVE

Bobby Sox Brigade

hey came marching over the hill after the war, brandishing cut-down clubs and whaling the ball with a merry ferocity. They wore shorts and pageboy haircuts, and remained unfazed when their exertions raised beads of glistening perspiration and turned their noses shiny.

Golf had long been one of the few socially acceptable forms of physical activity for girls and women. Mary Queen of Scots was an avid golfer who, according to legend, introduced the term "caddie" into the game's lexicon. Britain's Ladies Golf Union was formed in 1893. The first U.S. Women's Amateur was held in 1895, just one year after the formation of the U.S. Golf Association.

Golf soon became so popular among American women that a good many American men tried to keep them from playing it. They limited women's access to the country's few courses and warned of the dire consequences of overexertion. But women persisted, in some cases even forming their own clubs, until by the end of World War I women's golf had become an accepted albeit minor element of the nation's sports fabric.

But something changed after World War II, nationally and in Tulsa. Women weren't just tolerated on the golf course; they were encouraged.

Or, more specifically, their daughters were.

In 1949, six women convinced the Women's Oklahoma Golf Association to sponsor a junior program; a year later, the WOGA's first junior girls tournament was held at Tulsa Country Club, thus beginning the emergence of what *Tulsa World* golf writer Tom Lobaugh called "The Bobby Sox Brigade."

Four of the six founders of the junior girls program were Tulsans, including Tulsa Country Club member Irma Savage. The most passionate was Mabel Hotz, the wife of a Tulsa physician and an Oaks Country Club member. A mother of three daughters herself, Mabel Hotz became a sort of surrogate mother for the scores of girls who turned Oklahoma's junior program into one of the best in the nation over the next dozen years.

"I competed in a lot of junior tournaments because of Mabel," said Betsy Cullen, an entrant in that first junior tournament as an eleven-year-old, in a 2008 interview. "She'd call so many times that we'd finally laugh and say, 'Okay.'"

"She just had amazing energy."

The turnout for that first junior tournament was somewhat disappointing. Only eighteen girls showed up for qualifying. Jo Ann Grimes, whose father Oscar was one of TCC's best club players at the time, won medalist honors with a 92. Ann Ervine, seventeen-year-old daughter of Oaks greenskeeper Bob Ervine, beat Nancy Rawlinson of Muskogee in the finals for the championship.

Grimes came back to win the title in 1951, beginning a remarkable run for Tulsa Country Club youngsters. Over the next dozen years, Cullen won two junior and three state amateur titles and reached the semifinals of the 1955 national junior tournament, Patty David won two junior titles, and

Jeannie Thompson won three straight junior titles and the Trans-Miss.

Two other Tulsans, Sue Gail Dillman and Jill Kreager, also won junior titles during those years, and Dale Fleming—the future Dale McNamara—won the first three of her seven state amateur titles. And this at a time when the statewide competition included Muskogee's Beth Stone and Oklahoma City's Linda Melton Morse and Susie Maxwell Berning.

"We had such great competitions," said McNamara, now retired from coaching at the University of Tulsa. "Anybody who plays golf, and particularly at that level, can tell you that there's nothing more competitive. Particularly in match play. But we never had an unfriendly word at all."

In 1954, the fifteen-year-old Cullen turned Oklahoma women's golf upside down by defeating three-time defending state champion Margaret Williford 2-and-1 in the thirty-six-hole state amateur final at what was then Indian Hills Country Club. When Cullen won the women's title again in 1955—and Fleming won three of the next four years—some older golfers quietly lobbied to exclude the youngsters from the tournament. They lost that fight, too.

Thompson, who would add a state amateur title to her trophies in 1965, later moved to Oklahoma City, married Oklahoma's then-secretary of state John Rogers, and for a short time chaired the WOGA junior program.

A valedictory, of sorts, occurred in 1959 when Fleming defeated David, the reigning state junior champ, in the finals of the state amateur at Tulsa Country Club. David never came any closer to a state title; shockingly, she was killed in a 1962 car crash as she returned home from the University of Arkansas.

Dale Fleming McNamara won two of her seven state amateur titles on the TCC course and was instrumental in bringing the 1999 NCAA Division I women's championship to the club as well as the LPGA's Williams Championship. McNamara coached the University of Tulsa to four national championships during the 1980s.

Cullen dropped competitive golf for a while but came back to win her third state title in 1961 and went on to spend fourteen years on the LPGA Tour. She's been a successful teaching pro in Texas since the mid-1980s.

Cullen said she remembers her years at the club with great fondness.

"For us, it was pretty much our summer recreation," she said. "We would spend the afternoon at the swimming pool or playing touch football, and then in the evening my mother would bring dinner and we'd eat in the picnic area. This was before air conditioning, and other families would join us."

Fathers also seemed to be important to the postwar popularity of junior girls' golf. Lobaugh, in his report of June 1, 1950, noted with some surprise the number of "proud papas" who came to root for their daughters at the first state junior tournament.

The dedication of Cullen's father Ronald, an inveterate golfer who seemed to play regardless of weather or his own health, seemed to rub off on her.

"Ronald was somewhat impervious to weather," longtime member Forrest Shoemaker Jr. said in 2008. "Everybody else would have it hung up, and he'd be out there by himself.

"Everybody marveled, as he grew older and had some medical problems, how we wouldn't see him for a while and then, all of the sudden, he'd be back."

Betsy was the youngest of four daughters and the only one to really take golf seriously. The club's assistant pro, Sandy Francisco, handled the junior program and "really took an interest in me," Cullen said. No one objected when she used the rough along the old first fairway as a practice range.

"A boy named Johnny Zuniga, who was a classmate of mine, would shag for me," Cullen said. "He was a baseball player and always wanted to catch the ball in his cap. I never practiced as well when I went to a driving range as I did there because there was so little room for error.

"It was a wonderful place to grow up," said Cullen. "Gosh, I can remember playing four holes, taking a nap under a tree, and playing the next five. The caddies would look after you. The help in the kitchen. Great hamburgers. Great chocolate sundaes. And everybody played gin rummy."

Tulsa had been something of a haven for women golfers since at least the 1930s, when Tulsa Country Club was host to two state amateurs and players such as Estelle Drennan, Joyce Wallace, Ann Kennedy, and Patti Blanton established national reputations. The city's commitment to women's golf was rewarded in 1960, when the national junior and national women's amateur were played at Oaks and TCC on successive weeks in August. The events brought some of the game's stars—past, present, and future—to Tulsa, including Patty Berg, Ann Casey Johnstone, Sandra Haynie, Judy Eller, Carol Sorenson, Barbara McIntire, JoAnne Gunderson, and Mary Patton Janssen.

Unfortunately, the local talent did not distinguish itself. Jeannie Thompson and another Tulsan, state junior runner-up Suzy Marks, qualified for the junior championship flight at Oaks, but Marks lost in the first round and Thompson in the second. Sorenson, who would go on to win national collegiate championships as both a player and a coach at Arizona State and play on two Curtis Cup teams, defeated Sharon Fladoos for the title.

The only Oklahoman to survive two rounds of the women's amateur at Tulsa Country Club was TCC's Dottie Biddick. The irrepressible Gunderson, then a twenty-one-year-old Arizona State coed, won the second of five national amateur trophies with her usual color and good humor. Barely surviving a quarterfinal scare from future LPGA star Sandra

Tulsa Country Club's Dottie Biddick was the only local golfer to survive the first round of the 1960 U.S. Women's Amateur at TCC. She's pictured here with a trophy from the 1967 club championship.

Irrepressible JoAnne Gunderson shows off the hardware after winning the 1960 U.S. Women's Amateur at Tulsa Country Club. The Great Gundy, as she was known before marrying Don Carner, won five U.S. Amateurs and is the only woman to have won the USGA Junior championship, the U.S. Women's Amateur and the U.S. Women's Open.

Spuzich, Gunderson easily defeated her best friend Judy Eller in the semis and beat Jean Ashley of Chanute, Kansas, 6-and-5 in the final.

The Bobby Sox Brigade was a vanguard of change. In 1960, Tulsa Public Schools finally allowed girls to compete in the state high school golf tournament. Patty David, playing for Tulsa Central, won. A decade later, Dale Fleming McNamara took over the women's golf program at the University of Tulsa and built it into a national power. In 1999, TU and TCC hosted the NCAA division women's championship.

"Where women's golf is now," said McNamara, "is a world of difference from where it was then."

Robert Henry "Skee" Riegel was a golfing vagabond who pitched his tent for a few years in the camp of Tulsa Country Club pro Morrie Gravatt. Colorful and dashing, a former college football player and Army Air Corps flight instructor, Riegel hadn't taken up golf until his twenties.

Just six years later, in 1946, Riegel shattered the U.S. Amateur stroke-play record with a thirty-six-hole 136. He also won the Trans-Mississippi. In the 1947 U.S. Amateur, Riegel beat John Dawson in the fog at Pebble Beach and won two matches for the U.S. Walker Cup team. In 1948 he won both the Trans-Miss and Western amateurs. Top-flight amateurs were still celebrities then, and Riegel fit the part, right down to a Douglas Fairbanks Jr. moustache.

Somewhere along the way, possibly through Jug McSpaden, Riegel met Gravatt; when Riegel played poorly in the 1948 U.S. Amateur, he went to Gravatt for help. Soon Riegel was getting his mail in Tulsa and listing TCC as his home course.

Riegel's run continued. He was low amateur at the 1949 U.S. Open and again won two Walker Cup matches. In January 1951, at the age of thirty-four, he turned pro and four months later was the leader in the clubhouse at Augusta until Ben Hogan, still recovering from a near-fatal car wreck, shot a 68 to win his first Masters. Riegel finished eighth on the money list that year and won a shoe contract with Wilson.

Two years later, Riegel's Tour career was just about over. He left Tulsa at the end of 1953 to become head professional at the new Radnor Valley Country Club in Philadelphia, near his hometown of Upper Darby, Pennsylvania. He continued playing

Robert "Skee" Riegel was one of the nation's top amateurs when he moved to Tulsa and enlisted the advice of TCC head pro Morrie Gravatt. Riegel turned pro at the rather advanced age of thirty-four, enjoying a short but successful career.

money list, played on a Ryder Cup team, and won the 1952 Canadian Open and the 1954 Colonial. While at TCC, he won the 1957 Oklahoma Open at Twin Hills. According to one story, Palmer once bested Sam Snead with the help of a tee shot that veered off the course, hit a passing dump truck, and bounced back into the fairway.

Other top TCC players of the era included Walter Emery, Oscar Grimes, Harold Corbett, Bill McPartland, Mack McClure, and Bill Smith, who counted among his trophies a national left-handed championship. Another regular on the TCC course, although not yet a full member, was Jim Unruh, a young friend of Bill Smith's who would become the University of Tulsa's first scholarship golfer and a USGA official.

Corbett, as an eighteen-year-old, won the 1956 state amateur on the TCC course. Emery, in 1953, made one of his last real runs at the title.

Emery was fourteen years removed from his last state amateur title when the tournament came to TCC in May 1953. The favorite was defending champion Joe Walser Jr. The 1952 runner-up, Johnny Johnson,

the Masters, though, and made the cut eleven years in a row. Well past ninety, Riegel at last report was still occasionally hitting a few balls at a course near his home in Cape May, New Jersey.

Riegel was not Tulsa Country Club's only fine player during those years. Gravatt qualified for several U.S. Opens and won the 1948 South Central sectional. When a bad back forced Gravatt to give up golf in 1955, TCC hired laconic North Carolinian Johnny Palmer, who had finished as high as third on the Tour

This circa 1950s scorecard gives a statistical picture of the TCC course before it was reordered in the 1960s. The only recognizable name is that of Lee Hunt, a Tulsa businessman. Even with hefty handicaps, this foursome put up some nice round numbers.

51

was also in the field. Both were collegiate stars, Walser at Oklahoma State (then Oklahoma A&M) and Johnson at the University of Oklahoma.

Emery, by comparison, must have seemed like an old man who had been around forever. But he was only just past forty, and on the first day went out and shot a 73 to tie for medalist honors with another Tulsan, Earl Fennell.

Johnson fell by the wayside in the first round of match play, but Walser and most of the other top players advanced. Emery beat Oscar Grimes with a birdie on the eighteenth, and Fennell narrowly avoided defeat to budding sportscaster Mack Creager.

Double rounds the next day reduced the field to eight, including Walser, Emery, Fennell, Tulsa carpenter Leonard Young, and eighteen-year-old Fred Lawson, who had been medalist in the 1952 national caddie tournament.

Emery won his quarterfinal match 2-up and was leading his semifinal with Bill Parker by three holes with three to play when, inexplicably, he became unable to make even the shortest putt. He lost four straight holes, including a playoff, while missing two three-footers and an eight-footer.

It cannot be said the final was anticlimactic. The nineteen-year-old Parker scrambled out of danger time after time to stay even with the more experienced Young through thirty-four holes. But his last two tee shots went too far astray, and the steadier Young tapped in a couple of pars to win 1-up.

A record field of 219 signed up for the 1956 tournament at TCC, including defending champion and OSU star Ab Justice, national junior champion Billy "Cotton" Dunn of Duncan, national caddie champion Jerry Pittman of Tulsa, and a slew of past winners and almost-winners. But it was Corbett and Tulsa shoe salesman John Bridges who survived to give the tournament one of its most unlikely pair of finalists ever.

Bridges was the underdog in every match he played, barely survived the first round, and had to beat medalist Walt Melton in the quarterfinals. Corbett, a state high school champion from Cascia Hall, got through the first round with the help of an ace on what was then the par-3 fifth hole, but otherwise stayed under the radar all the way to the championship match.

Corbett won the first hole of the final and was never headed, winning 4-and-3.

Medalist in the national caddie tournament in 1952, Fred Lawson later teamed with Jim Unruh to give Tulsa Country Club one of the area's most formidable four-ball teams.

Most golf is played at less than the top level. For fun, you might say. You might say that, but it wouldn't be exactly true. The idea of making a shot or a hole or a match "a little more interesting" probably came along right after somebody thought of sewing feathers into a leather pouch and hitting it with a crooked stick.

One of the longest and certainly most complicated friendly games in the history of golf began at Tulsa Country Club just after World War II. Golfers of various abilities, known as "The Dogs," ventured forth daily in various combinations, competing under a Byzantine scoring system intended to keep winnings—and losses—spread thin.

The mastermind was Frank Gray, an old-time oilman who came to town in 1911 and for a number of years served as club secretary. After he retired in 1950, Gray and his wife Laurabelle worked more or less full time keeping track of the Dogs, logging all the pluses and minuses in an enormous ledger book that defied translation by even the most gifted cryptographer. Gray even had a separate phone line put in at the TCC clubhouse, listed under "Dogs," so that interested parties could check on the day's prospects.

"The phone was at his special table in the grillroom of the old TCC clubhouse," Tom Lobaugh wrote in 1976. "Many insisted Frank was sitting at that table and had the clubhouse built around him in 1917."

The normal procedure was for Gray to ask, "Will you go today?" when one of the Dogs walked into the grillroom, to which the standard reply was, "I'll go."

The phrase "Chinese New Year" scrawled on the chalkboard signaled it was time to pay up.

When Gray died in 1968, the rest of the pack discovered no one would take up his bookkeeping, not even for pay. They still played, but less often and under more simplified rules, until time eventually ran the remaining Dogs to ground, too.

A painting of Gray and his happy band still hangs in the men's locker room, a tribute to the spirit of camaraderie and fun that lies at the heart of a successful club, and makes life a little more interesting.

Country club membership had long been a symbol of status. To the children of the Depression suddenly awash in postwar prosperity, it may have been even more so. Certainly, Americans in the 1950s had more money and more inclination to spend it than ever before.

For John P. "Jack" Gallagher, an accountant with the firm of Warren and Godfrey, a Tulsa Country Club membership was particularly meaningful. His father, Patrick Henry Gallagher, had been TCC caddie master during the 1930s.

"That was a great goal of Dad's, to come back and be a member of that club," Jack Gallagher's son Pat Gallagher said in a 2008 interview.

"He was never a great golfer, but he was a great teacher. He had a lot of fun playing. A great weekend was to get together with some guys and go play golf, then come back in to the grill or the men's locker room and play gin rummy."

Gin rummy was very big. Poker, it seems, had been banned, but the gin rummy games ran almost continuously. Bridge was still popular, too, especially among women, and family bingo nights were a regular feature.

Pat Cremin, whose grandfather lived across the street from the first tee, lived in the neighborhood as a child and recalls a connection between Immaculate Conception, then the local parish, and the club.

"In the old days, you had a lot of people who lived in those hills and belonged to the club," Cremin said in 2007. "Many were members of that Catholic Church."

Tulsa Country Club may have been a model of 1950s placidness on the surface, but the very ground beneath it was shifting. Newer, more modern clubs were coming on line. Members and potential members lived farther and farther away. The old clubhouse, although much beloved, was turning into a bottomless money pit. And the possibility that the golf course might be sold out from under the membership remained a nagging possibility, even after a twenty-year lease extension was signed in 1953.

Then, at the end of November 1956, club president Lee Murdock suddenly announced an agreement had been reached to buy the course and some additional property from the Kennedy family for $325,000. The transaction involved a total of 149 acres: the original eighty, forty-two added in the expansion of the late 1910s, and a little over twenty-two acres formerly occupied by Jim Kennedy's public course and about five acres adjoining

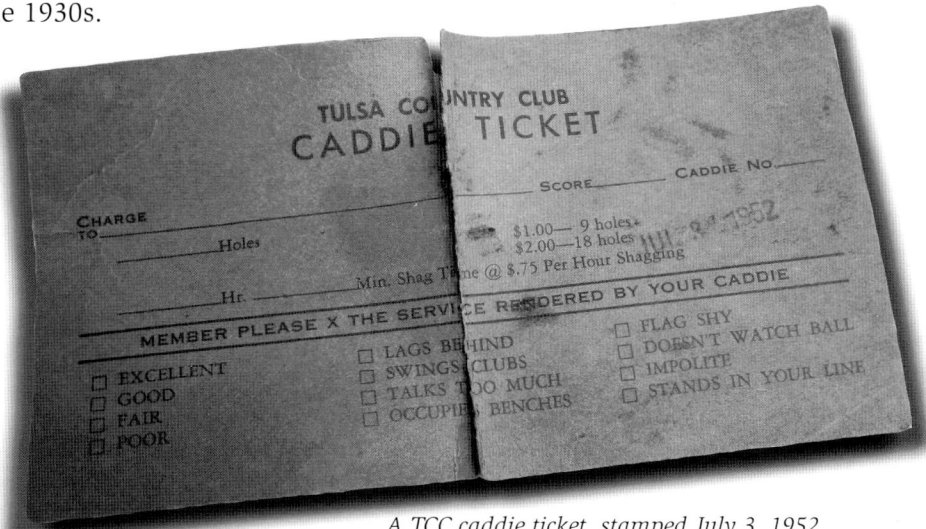

A TCC caddie ticket, stamped July 3, 1952.

Golf was not the only game enjoyed by Tulsa Country Club members during the 1950s—and not all club activities took place at TCC. Here Roger LaPlante tries his hand at horseshoes during a Women's Golf Association Husbands and Wives Party at Arrowhead Ranch near Skiatook. The "gallery," from left to right, is Orville Barnett, Chuck Benjamin, E. M. "Pete" Lofgren, Milt Griffith, and Dick Coiner.

the northwest corner of the TCC course. The deal also included the old Kennedy clubhouse, which was soon demolished.

All of this was to be added to the seven-plus acres occupied by the clubhouse, parking lot, and pro shop, and already owned by the club.

The acquisition didn't just put an end to speculation about the future of the course. It signaled a quite literal change of direction for the club. Murdock, in remarks to the local newspapers, said long-range plans included a new clubhouse "at the crest of a hill on the west side of the property."

The old clubhouse, for all of its charm, was proving to be enormously expensive to maintain and increasingly inadequate for the club's needs. Air conditioning had been added to the grillroom, dining room and ballroom in 1950. Almost $150,000 was spent three years later for locker rooms at the swimming pool, a major upgrade of the kitchen, paving, and a fairway sprinkler system. Plans for a new wing were dropped because of the cost in May 1956. That same year, the Elks Lodge briefly considered making an offer for the property.

The club leadership seems to have vacillated on the matter, perhaps in part because of a bylaw passed in 1953 limiting directors to two consecutive terms. The club had six presidents during the 1950s, although one—M. D. Gilbert—served only a few days before resigning because of a move to Kansas City. Murdock served four years (1950 and 1956–58) and Tom Riggin, elected by the board to replace Gilbert, just short of three. Fred Robbins and L. C. "Bud" Woods each served one year.

Murdock and Riggin seem to have been particularly favorable to the idea of a new clubhouse. In February 1958, at the annual membership meeting, Murdock disclosed the clubhouse was going to be appraised for possible sale. According to minutes of a board meeting held a week later, on February 25, "A general discussion toward the possibility of selling the old clubhouse and the building of a new club house [sic] on the west side of the golf course was the main topic of the evening."

But the club was having cash-flow problems, and nothing seems to have been done for another year. In January 1959 the board recommended a $400,000 "building expansion and remodeling" program, but it doesn't seem to have gone anywhere. In April, a building committee chaired by Charles Gannaway Jr., was appointed to "consider three alternatives: extensive remodeling, a new clubhouse on the west side of the course and no action." In July, a second committee was formed to look into the financial aspects of the situation. In October the sale of the existing clubhouse was again discussed.

Still nothing happened.

The decision in January 1960 to look into the possibility of getting a national hotel chain to build a combination clubhouse and hotel created a lot of excitement, but less than a month later Woods told the annual membership meeting the proposal was "premature."

But the matter was far from settled. Tulsa Country Club was on a distinctly new tack. Jim Kennedy, largely responsible for negotiating the course buyout, was given a plaque and a bronze lifetime membership card in 1957. The Kennedys were paid off in 1958. The club was moving on—and, like the rest of the nation, would find the kaleidoscopic '60s to be a decade of revolutionary change.

Themed soirees have remained a staple of country club life. These women and their stiff friend are planning something called the Calypso Party.

Fashion shows were an important part of the club's social scene. Here Mrs. John Elder, Mrs. Dan Rodricks, and Mrs. Jack Bredouw plan an "Easter Parade."

*Donald Honn was a nationally known architect when
TCC commissioned him to design a new clubhouse in 1966.
Among Honn's creations was the Lortondale addition.*

CHAPTER SIX

New Direction

Tulsa County Club members drove through a two-inch snowfall to reach their clubhouse on the night of February 21, 1966. After years of talking, committee meetings, and false starts, they were being asked for a decision both long dreaded and eagerly anticipated. They were being asked to leave behind the old mansion on Country Club Road.

The vote that night was not taken lightly. The board of directors, led by President Tom Riggin, proposed a $900,000 clubhouse and pro shop, along with a new swimming pool and tennis courts, on the west side of the club property. The move and even the building itself, a modernist design by award-winning local architect Donald Honn, represented a complete break with tradition. The venerable Tillinghast course would, in effect, be turned 180 degrees on its axis. The old clubhouse and its three generations of bridge tournaments, wedding receptions, holiday dances, jingling slot machines, and perpetual Calcuttas was to be sold for whatever could be had—and the prospects suggested that might not be much.

But nostalgia was not in vogue, in Tulsa or anywhere else, in 1966. It was a year of change in the middle of a decade of change—a decade that marched on Washington and flew to the moon, fought in the streets of America's cities and in southeast Asia, wore its hair long and its skirts short. It was the decade of Henry Mancini and Mick Jagger, George Wallace and Martin Luther King Jr., *Mary Poppins* and *Midnight Cowboy*.

So Tulsa Country Club joined the trend. On that snowy night in February, it left tradition behind and struck out in a new direction.

The 1960s began much as the 1950s ended, with unprecedented prosperity creating what economist John Kenneth Galbraith called a new age of affluence. The nation's real gross domestic product grew more than 50 percent during the 1960s; so, perhaps not coincidentally, did the number of golf courses. Overall spending on recreation more than doubled. Two of every three automobiles worldwide were parked in American driveways.

For America's country clubs, a burgeoning economy was proving to be not without drawbacks. For, even as club membership grew, operating costs grew faster. Wages skyrocketed, and many clubs found themselves facing decades of deferred maintenance and outmoded facilities. A *Wall Street Journal* story near the end of 1961 reported country club costs had risen 45 percent in just seven years despite a membership increase of a half-million nationwide.

Tulsa Country Club, as mentioned previously, opened the decade by playing host to the national women's amateur. The following year, TCC's Betsy Cullen returned to competitive golf and won the state women's title on Bartlesville's Hillcrest course, beating Sue Maxwell 4-and-3 in the final.

In 1962, TCC pulled off a rare double by claiming both the men's and women's Trans-Miss champions. Jeannie Thompson, at only seventeen, and Bob Ryan, a twenty-two-year-old Air Force lieutenant on leave from pilot training, each came from deep in the pack to win as long shots.

Ryan had won a state junior title and played with some distinction for Cascia Hall and the University of Oklahoma, but attracted so little attention during qualifying at the 1962 men's Trans-Miss at St. Louis' Warson Country Club that he was not even mentioned in early press coverage of the event. Most of the ink went to Oklahoma City's Richard Norville, whose thirty-six-hole 144 took medalist honors by two shots over two others, including Oklahoma State University standout George Hixon.

Norville, it so happened, had beaten Ryan in the first round of the Oklahoma state open the previous week. Nothing the first two days suggested Ryan would make a run at Norville or any of the other tournament's big names. His 156 in qualifying put him in the middle of the championship flight, and he remained largely unnoticed until the semifinals, when he stunned Walker Cupper Bob Cochran.

Ryan was three down through eight holes of that match when a heavy downpour interrupted play. When the match resumed, he won four of the first five holes as the more experienced Cochran became visibly upset by a "hassle" over Ryan's use of his putter to smooth out spike marks on the tenth hole.

Cochran pulled himself together enough to draw back even, but on eighteen Ryan used his putter to run in a sixty-foot birdie from a waterlogged sand trap to win 1-up.

The next day's thirty-six-hole final over the University of Houston's Harry Toscano Jr. was just as close and just as strange.

Already two down, Ryan skied his second shot of the twenty-seventh hole over the green, off a cart trail, and onto an outdoor dance floor. The dance floor was ruled an immovable obstruction, and Ryan was allowed a drop on the grass in front of the structure. From there, he hit the ball to within four feet of the pin and knocked down the putt to halve the hole with a par.

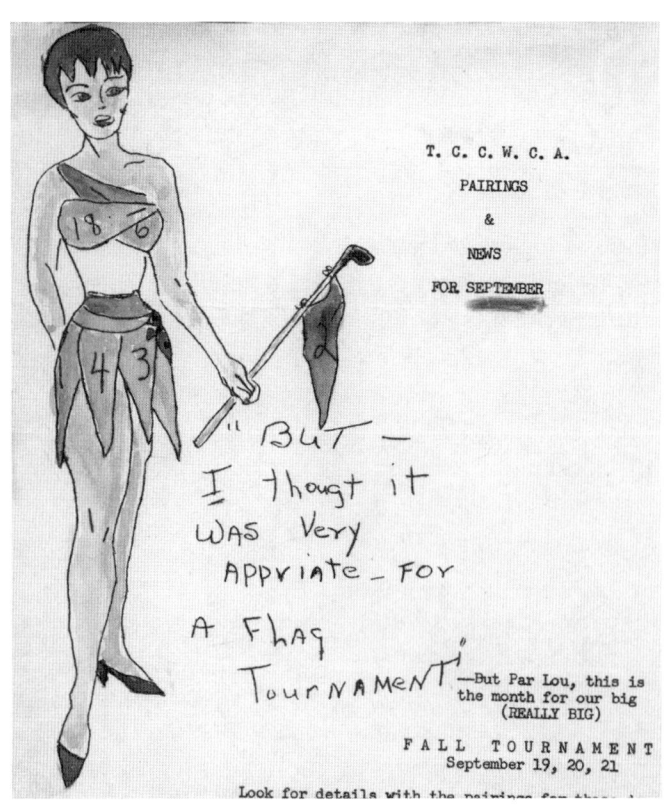

Ditzy "Par Lou" regularly adorned the newsletters and circulars of the TCC Women's Golf Association during the 1960s.

Ryan won the next four holes and held on for a 1-up victory as Toscano narrowly missed birdie putts on three of the last four holes.

The women's Trans-Miss was played the following week at the Wichita Country Club. Thompson had won her third straight state junior girls' just a few days earlier at Southern Hills, birdieing the first playoff hole after leading 3-up with four to play in regulation, and she shot a respectable 79 in qualifying at Wichita.

But Thompson was not among the favorites. The field included four Curtis Cup players—among them the legendary Ann Casey Johnstone—future U.S. Open champions Sandra Spuzich and Sandra Palmer, and Oklahoma City's Sue Maxwell. The medalists were former national junior champion Carol Jo Skala and five-time Kansas state champion Natasha Fife.

But Thompson was sharp and advanced rather easily through the first two match play rounds. In the third round she beat Curtis Cupper Clifford Ann Creed 3-and-2, then survived her closest match of the tournament with a fifteen-foot birdie putt on No. 17 to beat Kathy Farrar, 2-and-1.

That put Thompson into the semifinals, where she faced Ruth White Miller of Long Beach, California. In a match similar to the state junior girls' final, Miller won the seventeenth and eighteenth holes to force a playoff, but Thompson birdied the second playoff hole to reach the finals against Johnstone.

Johnstone had won the tournament in 1959 and finished second two years before that, but could not keep up with her youthful opponent.

"Consistently outdriving her veteran opponent and playing more steadily, the 110-pound Tulsa youngster never trailed in the scheduled 36-hole match," reported the Associated Press.

When Johnstone three-putted the thirty-fourth hole, Thompson claimed victory, 3-and-2.

Youth, then, was served in the 1962 Trans-Miss tournaments. It would become a recurring theme in the years ahead. America was getting younger—literally. A population tidal wave with no memory of the Great Depression or World War II was sweeping forward with incalculable force, washing away the past, and forever altering the landscape.

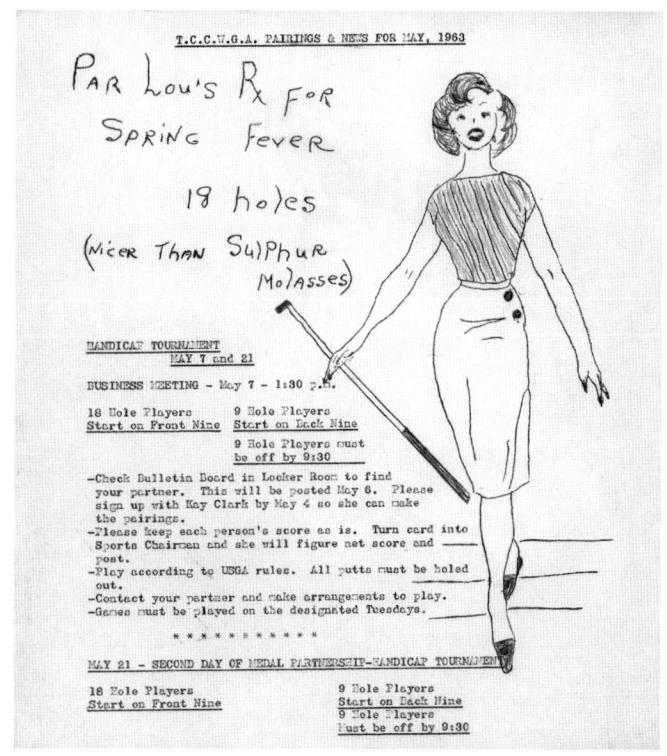

The last state tournament played on the old Tulsa Country Club layout began one of the most remarkable two-year runs ever for an Oklahoma golfer.

At twenty-one, Bob Dickson had already played in eleven state men's amateurs when the 1965 tournament came to Tulsa Country Club. Tall, broad-shouldered, and long-limbed, he nevertheless seemed at first glance an unlikely mauler because of the mild, owlish eyes gazing out from behind enormous spectacles. But when Big Bob got it going, no one in the state could play with him.

Dickson had grown up on golf courses in McAlester and Muskogee where his father and brother, both named Ben Dickson, were club professionals. Ben Jr. had won the 1954 state amateur, and Bob had almost done the same in 1964, losing narrowly to George Hixon at Oklahoma City's Twin Hills.

He got off to a solid but not great start at TCC, shooting a 71 to trail by two after the first round. On the second day, though, Dickson potted a 67 that included five birdies and a bogey. That gave him a three-shot lead on eighteen-year-old Charles Weinshilboum of Ponca City.

A 70 for the third round doubled his lead to six shots over David Hines, a two-time state high school champion from Tulsa Hale who had managed an opening-round 69.

Dickson attacked the course on his last round like Sherman through Georgia, birdieing the first two holes and leading by eight through six. Then, on seven, his tee shot strayed into tall rough on the right and he needed two whacks with a five iron to get it out. The resulting double-bogey blunted Dickson's attack, and he continued to hit tee shots and approaches hither and yon the rest of the round.

But his putter saved him. Dickson needed only twenty-nine putts to salvage a one-over 73 and win the tournament by five shots, the most since the tournament went to stroke play.

"I feel lucky to break 80," Dickson said happily, then celebrated with a Grapette over vanilla ice cream and Coca-Cola.

Things were not quite so jolly less than two months later. Dickson, in the hunt for the U.S. Amateur championship at Southern Hills, discovered an extra club in his bag on the second hole of the final round and was penalized four strokes. He lost to Bob Murphy by one.

But Dickson seemed unfazed. He won the state amateur again in 1966, and then in 1967 became the first man since Lawson Little beat Walter Emery in the 1935 U.S. Amateur finals to win the American and British amateur championships in the same year. Dickson turned professional in 1968 and played nine years on the pro tour, but a bad back and an erratic driver kept him from recapturing the feel of those sun-splashed summers of the mid-1960s.

Donald Honn was a no-frills kind of guy. In the tradition of Louis Sullivan and Frank Lloyd Wright, he was an architect who believed ardently in the modernist principles. Form should follow function. Ornamentation should be left to Christmas trees. The approach made Honn quite successful and very well known.

An Illinois native trained at the University of Illinois, Honn arrived in Tulsa in 1949 to serve as a consulting engineer on the U.S. Jaycee World Headquarters building being erected on Twenty-first Street near the east bank of the Arkansas River. He soon earned a reputation for innovative and economical designs ranging from low-cost prefab housing to showy upscale oil mansions. When he was awarded the commission for Tulsa Country Club's new clubhouse in 1966, he had a string of nearly two-dozen awards to his credit.

By odd coincidence, as it turned out, his most lauded creation had involved a golf course—the old Meadowbrook Country Club (then routinely referred to as the "Jewish Country Club") east of South Yale Avenue between Twenty-sixth Street and Twenty-seventh Place.

Developer Howard Grubb bought the property in the early 1950s and hired Honn to design an entire subdivision of distinctive yet affordable houses. The result was Lortondale, the first housing addition in the United States with central heat and air and the first in Tulsa with a neighborhood swimming pool. The houses featured open floor plans and liberal use of glass and stone. Most sold for less than $13,000, well within the means of a growing middle class.

Honn and his family even moved into Lortondale, living for many years at 4940 East Twenty-sixth Street in a house still in use. *Better Homes and Gardens* featured the home in its May 1957 issue.

"This home breaks away from stilted pattern in a lively and refreshing way," wrote architect John Normile.

A 1959 article in the same publication lauded Honn's Lortondale homes.

"These homes use every square foot—and there's more than one use for most areas," it said.

Grubb and Honn were honored at the National Association of Homebuilders convention—and wound up with contracts for hundreds more houses all over the southwestern United States.

Honn also designed larger and more upscale projects, including homes at 106 East Twenty-fifth Street and 2272 East Thirty-fourth Street. A house southeast of Bartlesville owned by Cities Service executive P. M. Arnold was named one the nation's three best new homes by the American Institute of Architects in 1958. Honn also designed his own office building, still standing at 3208 East Twenty-first Street, and the "new" Meadowbrook Country Club clubhouse southeast of Tulsa.

Honn's concept for Tulsa Country Club fit in perfectly with his existing body of work and the architectural tenor of the times. Among additions to Tulsa's skyline during the mid-to-late-1960s were the Fourth National Bank Tower (now Bank of America Building), the Oral Roberts University campus, the Tulsa International Airport passenger terminal, and a new civic center, including a high-rise city hall, a convention center, and a central library. At the same time, many older buildings were demolished or abandoned, including the Hotel Tulsa, the Medical and Dental Arts Building, and the American Airlines Building.

A second-generation TCC member, Forrest Shoemaker Jr. has been president of the club twice, in 1970 and again in 1990.

By definition, the architecture of the 1960s rejected the past.

This created a problem for Honn and just about every other architect designing clubhouses during those years. They wanted to be modern, innovative, and forward-looking. Country clubs, on the other hand, tend to be conservative places, steeped in tradition and comfortable with the past. So, while no one should have been surprised when Honn proposed a sprawling, single-story structure different in just about every way from TCC's existing clubhouse—and from just about every other clubhouse in the country—it did not engender universal approval. Some people just felt like a clubhouse should look like a clubhouse.

"This building had a lot of criticism," recalled Forrest Shoemaker Jr., whose family had belonged to TCC since the 1930s. "Some people referred to it as a train depot."

There were other problems. Originally budgeted at $900,000, the building's estimated cost jumped to $1 million before construction even began in the fall of 1966. And, it fell far behind schedule. The club had hoped to open the new building in the fall of 1967, but it would be the following spring before it was ready for use.

But when the new clubhouse did open in March 1968, it was to considerable excitement.

"The sprawling, palatial [sic] new Country Club, a dream of many years for members, will be taking the spotlight much of this month," proclaimed the *Tulsa World* in a February 29 full-page layout featuring more than a half-dozen members modeling clothes for a planned fashion show.

The big event came in mid-March, with a weekend-long soiree.

"Those who attended the weekend celebration could dance (and dine!) Friday, Saturday and Sunday evening in the elegant new clubhouse on the west side of the old and famous golf course," the *World*'s Julie Blakely wrote a few days later.

"Members gathered to inspect the smart new furniture and the handsome draperies put in place just minutes before the party began," Blakely continued.

The club's choice of music may say something about its attachment to tradition. In the Age of Aquarius, the new ballroom resonated to the big band sounds of the Tommy Dorsey Orchestra—twelve years after Tommy Dorsey himself died.

"The men were handsome in dinner jackets," wrote Blakely. "The women's selection of gowns ranged from short brown lace to formal gowns that almost swept the posh carpeting."

Everyone said Don Ryan "looks like Ronald Reagan," Blakely reported.

Louis and Ernestine Valdez "seldom missed a dance."

The clubhouse has seen a good deal of dancing and dining over the past forty years. Its view of downtown Tulsa has become the club's trademark. In retrospect, it is easy to see that the current clubhouse was as much a reflection of 1968 as the old clubhouse was of 1916. And that, on the whole, it has weathered the years and changing fashion better than many of its contemporaries.

"I always thought Donald Honn took a lot of flak unfairly," said Shoemaker. "This was the type of building he designed and everybody knew it. And it has been a very functional building, actually."

When the clubhouse plans were disclosed in February 1966, treasurer E. L. Stucker confidently declared there would be no problem paying for it.

"We have been planning this building for three years," Stucker told the *Tulsa Tribune*.

The same, apparently, could not be said for the golf course. For reasons never fully explained, very little money was set aside for the realignment necessitated by the new clubhouse. The *World*'s Lobaugh, in July 1967, said the club was to meet with prolific Oklahoma City course architect Floyd Farley, but little if anything seems to have come from it. Texas-based Joe Finger, who had recently finished Dallas's Los Colinas Country Club and was working on Tulsa's Cedar Ridge, was thought to be a possibility until TCC officers found out how much he would cost.

So they turned to Jim Unruh, a recent addition to the club who had played many of the nation's top courses.

Jim Unruh won the first of seven club championships in 1967. He also served as club president in 1970. A topflight amateur for decades, Unruh is a member of the U.S. Golf Association's rules committee.

"They said they'd contacted some architects and they couldn't afford them," Unruh said in a 2008 interview. "They said, 'Can you design the course?' I said I could, but I couldn't build the greens. So I asked a local landscaper named Joe Seibert to help me, and it worked out fine."

Unruh started by getting some information on Tillinghast. The old Mad Master was as out of fashion as spats in the mid-1960s. Better equipment and stronger players put more of a premium on distance and less on iron play.

"He didn't like par-5s," said Unruh, "so he put them back-to-back to get them out of the way."

"He liked narrow fairways, rarely used fairway bunkers, and his greens sloped toward you off the tee. His first holes were usually short."

Under the new alignment, No. 16 became No. 1. As laid out by Unruh, the new No. 1 featured a big tree smack dab in the middle of the fairway that caused a considerable amount of grief before it was removed. At one point, disgruntled golfers hung Unruh in effigy from a particularly offending limb. But, says Unruh, the obstacle mimicked other Tillinghast courses.

"He liked trees in the middle of the fairway," Unruh said.

A breakdown of the "old" and "new" course:

New	Old
1	16
2	17
3	18
4	1
5	7
6	8
7	9
8	10
9	11
10	12
11	13
12	3
13	4
14	5
15	6
16	2
17	14
18	15

The first big tournament on the new layout was the fiftieth state women's amateur. Played the first week of June 1968—a week in which Robert Kennedy was assassinated, enemy artillery shelled Saigon, and a little known Texas congressman named George Herbert Walker Bush was touted as a running mate for President Nixon—the tournament field of 178 included six former champions. Among them were four-time champions Patti Blanton and Margaret Williford, three-time champions Linda Melton Morse and Dale Fleming McNamara, and defending champion Lucy Beeler.

"The ladies who haven't played TCC since the state tourneys of 1959 or 1948 will find most of the holes the way they remember them—except the numbers have been changed," said the June 2 *Tulsa World*.

"New tees have been built for the first hole, and what is now the 18th. A new trap has just been completed for the lake hole (now No. 6)."

The new alignment shortened the course by 185 yards for ladies and shaved a stroke off par.

"Through heavy air and on greens dampened by high humidity," as the *World*'s Bill Crawley put it, Morse shot a 75 to win the qualifying round by three strokes over McNamara and six over Jeannie Thompson. Transplanted to Tulsa, Morse had missed the 1967 tournament because of back surgery. But, on this particular day, Crawley said she demonstrated no ill effects of the injury that had nagged Morse much of her playing career.

"Her irons were sharp, her woods accurate, and, even more impressive because of her layoff from competitive golf, her short game was superb," Crawley wrote.

Unfortunately for Morse, McNamara was even sharper.

McNamara was really challenged only once, by Muskogee's Susan Basolo in the semifinals, and was three-over for the week. She beat Thompson 8-and-7 in the final.

The *Tulsa Tribune*'s Jay Cronley called McNamara's 6-and-5 defeat of Rinda Koppits "one of the finest rounds of golf in the 50-year history of the state tournament."

"Dale was four under par, did not miss a fairway, birdied four par-5 holes and was putting for eagle inside 10 feet on three of the greens. She missed two greens but was on the fringe of both."

"You might not believe it," said Koppits, "but I was hitting the ball really well. That was the best round I've had, and I was beaten 6-and-5."

Said McNamara after the final: "I've never played better in my life."

In some ways, life at Tulsa Country Club during the 1960s went on much as it had before. Bus trips to football games in Norman and Stillwater. Summer days at the pool. Teas and luncheons and moments of hijincks with the likes of the "Tulsa Country Club Dixieland Swing Beatdown Philharmonic Jazz Orchestra." There was an annual members' tournament involving mannequins.

But internal and external forces did take a toll. At a time when country clubs in general were falling out of favor with an increasingly informal and anti-establishment generation, TCC found itself stretched, financially and emotionally, by the move to the new clubhouse. The result, in the end, was a drastic change in the way club members viewed leadership.

For most of its existence, Tulsa Country Club's board of directors had been headed by a small group of men (and they were all men). Most board presidents served for years on end—as many as eleven in the case of E. H. Leroux. Between 1937 and 1967, four men—E. H. Leroux, F. Lee Murdock, Tom Riggin, and Fred Robbins—led the club for all but four years. They had done yeoman work, but by the late 1960s a conviction took hold that the club needed broader participation from its members.

"In the forties, fifties, and sixties, the club operated differently than it does now," said Forrest Shoemaker Jr. "There was a small group running the club who had control of the board. This group decided what should be done and everyone went along with it."

F. P. "Dude" Mueller, 1972 club president, and his wife Elaine in a 1986 photo. Mueller helped guide the club through difficult financial times after the construction of the current clubhouse.

In 1968, C. Page Stanley began a series of single-term presidencies that has remained consistent to the present time. Paul Vaananen, Forrest Shoemaker Jr., and Jim Unruh followed Stanley.

"When we moved into the new clubhouse, there was trouble with the contractor. The usual things," said Unruh. "Finances were a big problem. Forrest Shoemaker, myself, and Vaananen, who was a vice president at Skelly, we had our work cut out for us. We were fighting membership loss, the economy, and everything else, but we got it straightened out."

Geographically, Tulsa almost tripled in size during the 1960s. The freeway system that took shape during the decade sped the outward migration of the city's population, especially to the south and southeast. Attempts to develop the areas around Tulsa Country Club met with middling success at best.

According to Shoemaker, there was another direction Tulsa Country Club could have gone during the 1960s. Instead of building the new clubhouse, he said, TCC could have gone in with the new Cedar Ridge club then in the organization stages.

"At that time, Cedar Ridge was being formed up," he said. "It was offered up that the TCC membership could be moved to the new club on the south side. But the group in charge was not in favor of that."

And so, in the era of change, Tulsa Country Club stayed put, old and at the same time new, completely different and yet somehow the same.

Trays depicting the TCC course layout were produced in the early 1960s. Some, like this one, bore the names of specific club events. Others simply said "Tulsa Country Club."

A dance in the current clubhouse shortly after the move.

The Par Fiesta was a popular Women's Golf Association event for many years, including several when it involved a roving mannequin.

CHAPTER SEVEN

Tulsa's Downtown Country Club

David Thompson didn't know all that much about Tulsa or about country clubs. But, like a lot of the young executives moving to Tulsa in the early 1970s, he had taken up golf and wanted to find a place to play. Someone suggested he try Tulsa Country Club.

"He said he thought I could get some kind of golf-only membership," Thompson remembers.

TCC's membership chairman, Burt Gilliam, told Thompson no such category existed. But, he said, the club had recently begun offering something that might be of interest. With its membership aging and more and more young families heading for the suburbs, TCC had reinstituted a junior member program featuring a low initiation fee and reduced monthly dues assessed on a sliding age scale.

"I think it was $200 for the initiation fee, and the dues were something like seventeen dollars a month," Thompson said. "And I had to look real closely to see if I could afford that seventeen dollars."

Thompson was one of the club's two junior members when he joined in 1970. He was twenty-five. As he remembers it, the average member was about sixty-five.

David Thompson joined the club in 1970. He was elected president of TCC in 2008.

That changed dramatically over the next decade. Despite the migration to suburbia, Tulsa Country Club's membership grew larger and younger, due in large measure to the club's ability to market itself to both downtown workers and young families.

Thompson's experience was no doubt similar to many others.

"At the time, I joined primarily to play golf," he said. "But, my daughter was about a year old and pretty soon it became more of a family deal. My daughter will be thirty-nine in a month or so, but she still comes back here every year and brings her kids for the Fourth of July at the club."

That was the Tulsa of the 1970s: young families and Fourth of July fireworks.

Not that there weren't problems. Tulsa was subject to the same social tensions afflicting the rest of the country. But most of them seemed to be addressed in a manner that defused the more volatile situations.

It helped that the town was flourishing. Energy remained strong. Tulsa's growing aerospace industry was building many of the components for the U.S. space program. American Airlines shipped jobs and employees in from New York and New Jersey. The city's highway system and the Tulsa Port of Catoosa were nearing completion.

In 1971, The Williams Companies and a Chicago developer announced plans to tear out nine square blocks of downtown's notorious skid row and erect in its place the state's tallest building, a fifty-two-floor tower designed by Minorui Yamasaki, architect of New York's World Trade Center. Eventually, the project would include a luxury hotel and a performing arts center, also designed by Yamasaki, on the site of the old Hotel Tulsa. The following year, *Forbes* magazine ranked Tulsa as one of America's most livable cities.

Tulsa Country Club was not about to get left behind.

The men's state amateur returned to Tulsa Country Club in late June 1973. The course had changed considerably in the eight years since TCC had last hosted the tournament, and not only because of the reordering of the holes. Six of them had been significantly altered.

Most noticeable was the new No. 3—the old No. 18. Some big trees that for decades guarded the approach had been lost in a storm and replaced with a bunker. Tees and greens had been rebuilt on several other holes, and "strategically placed bunkers in some of the driving impact areas will punish inaccuracy off the tees," the *World*'s Tom Lobaugh warned on June 24 in advance of the tournament.

Something else that had changed since 1965: the growing prominence of collegiate golf. Long popular in Oklahoma, by 1973 the college game had become the primary training ground for touring pros and many of the top club amateurs. Most of the favorites in the '73 state amateur came directly from the NCAA championships—won for the third straight year by Texas's Ben Crenshaw—played the previous week at Stillwater Country Club. Those included Oral Roberts University's Dave Barr, Brigham Young's Joey Dills, North Texas's Steve Dodson (a Tulsa native), and Oklahoma State's Henry DeLozier, the defending champion.

DeLozier had to withdraw after nine holes because of illness, but the other collegians put on a good show.

So did the TCC course.

Dills was the only player to make par on the first day, and that was achieved despite four-putting No. 11. Dodson and Barr, a burly Canadian who had finished fifth in the NCAA tournament, were two shots back.

Known mostly for his distance off the tee, Barr took the lead on the second day with his short game. He hit only seven fairways but made fifteen greens and parred two of the three he missed for a scrambling, one-under 71 that gave him a two-shot lead over the University of Tulsa's Craig Minnich.

"I felt like I was shooting a 76," Barr said afterward. "I couldn't hit any shots at all."

Barr birdied the first and last holes of the third round for an even-par 72, good enough to extend his lead to three shots over Dills. He promised not to back off going into the final eighteen holes.

"You ease up," Barr said, "and pretty soon, your lead is gone."

The only threat to Barr on the last day was his temper. An adverse ruling on the sixth green cost him a two-stroke penalty—and almost caused him to walk off the course.

"It got me a little steamy," Barr told Lobaugh. "I still don't think it was right."

Two of the players in Barr's foursome, Hank Edwards and Terry Wilkerson, said Barr "croqueted" a short putt on six. Barr disagreed. Dodson, the fourth member of the foursome, said he didn't see what happened. Under the circumstances, tournament officials decided they had no alternative but to assess the penalty. It turned an already bad hole for Barr into a triple-bogey that took him from two under to one over. Learning after the ninth hole that the decision was final, Barr proceeded to bogey ten and eleven before calming down enough to finish with a 74. With the rest of the field fading in a steady rain, that gave Barr a three-over-par 291 and an eight-shot victory over Edwards.

Only four subpar rounds were recorded during the week, with Wilkerson's third-round 70 the best. Just as it had many times in the past, Tillinghast's holes had proved a worthy test of golf—no matter the order in which they were played.

On the same days that the 1973 state amateur was being played at Tulsa Country Club, a young lawyer in the Nixon White House named John Dean tied the president to the 1972 break-in at the Democratic Headquarters in Washington's Watergate office complex. David Boren, a little-known legislator from Seminole, told the downtown Kiwanis Club that it was time for citizens to "get down out of the bleachers and get involved."

Most Tulsans, though, were probably more concerned about the news that, for the first time since World War II, the United States was contemplating a form of gasoline rationing. Oil and natural gas were both in short supply, leading to widespread suspicion of industry collusion. Frank Ikard, president of the American Petroleum Institute, angrily denied the charges and blamed environmental regulations and skyrocketing demand for dry gas pumps and high prices.

All of this was before the Arab members of the Organization of Petroleum Exporting Countries—OPEC—embargoed oil shipments to the United States, Japan, and much of Europe in retaliation for support of Israel in the Yom Kippur War. Lasting from October 1973 through the first three months of 1974, the embargo quadrupled oil prices and drove gasoline up from about thirty-eight cents a gallon to fifty-five. Even then, inventories were so tight that filling stations often limited sales to a few gallons, and a voluntary rationing system went into effect. Speed limits were lowered to fifty-five miles per hour. Inflation accelerated. And in November, Nixon announced an energy policy he said would make the United States independent of foreign oil by 1980.

But for the oil and gas sectors of Tulsa's economy—and Oklahoma's—the energy crisis was a boon. Tulsa thrived through most of the 1970s, and so did Tulsa Country Club.

"At that time, they were in a kind of growing stage," said Tim Leslie, who came to the club as assistant pro in 1974 and became head pro two years later. "We actually filled up to five hundred members plus a waiting list. I think we maxed out at 35,000 rounds of golf a year, which was unheard of."

The club's proximity to downtown was its biggest initial draw, one that attracted individuals as well as major employers who bought multiple memberships for their executives and wrote them off as business expenses.

Somewhere along the way, TCC picked up the slogan "Tulsa's Downtown Country Club." No one now seems to know exactly when the phrase was coined or by whom, but it fit.

"Many of the members worked downtown," said Forrest Shoemaker Jr. "They were able to play golf because it was close to work."

And he was one of them.

"I could come out at lunch and practice for thirty minutes," he said.

But, Shoemaker is quick to add, "We've always continued to work to be a family country club. Our intention was not to become a men's club."

Still, the men's grill remained the club's inner sanctum during the days before the Internal Revenue Service put an end to the "three-martini" business lunch.

"The room where the exercise equipment is now was the men's grill, and just about any day you went in there, it was full," Thompson said. "They always had a pot of bean soup going, and I'm pretty sure all they did was add beans and water from one day to the next."

He has particularly fond memories of three businessmen who seemed to practically live on the golf course: Roy Miegs, George Battles, and Toby Sanders.

Sanders was a manufacturers representative for an industrial supply company called DoAll. Battles was a crusty retired Halliburton executive. Miegs owned two stores that specialized in salvage merchandise. The stores were called Roy's No. 1 and Roy's No. 2 and sat side-by-side on South Harvard Avenue.

"Toby was one of these guys who always had a cigar in his mouth, and if he laughed on the golf course, you could hear him from one end to the other," Thompson said.

One day, on No. 10, Miegs pulled out a five wood he said he'd bought just for this particular hole. His tee shot went into the water, and Miegs broke the new club over his knee.

"Toby quietly gets the club out of the trash can, takes it out to Mohawk Park to Gene Roop, which was one of the few places in town you could get a club repaired, and the next day pulls it out on No. 10 and says, 'I bought this club just for this hole.'"

There were some bumps during these years. A club manager died unexpectedly. Several superintendents came and went. Buddy Phillips, who came to the club as head pro in 1968, soon left for Cedar Ridge. His replacement, Buddy Cook, also left after only a few years, in this case to return to Texas where he became a successful golf course developer.

In the late 1970s and early 1980s, Dutch elm disease ravaged the club as it did all of Tulsa, causing some eighty trees to be replaced.

Convention also took its lumps. The club tried to preserve tradition, but standards were changing.

Entertainer Roy Clark hosted a celebrity golf tournament to benefit a local children's hospital for several years before lending his name to a senior event in 1984. A former TCC member, Clark was known as an enthusiastic golfer and first-rate locker room raconteur.

"You had to wear a jacket in the dining room," Thompson said. "There were always these jackets in the coat room in case you got to the club without one. They were always the ugliest things you could imagine, probably as an incentive for you to remember to wear your own."

Undoubtedly, the most egregious breach of the dress code occurred one day while some of the older female club members were playing bridge next to the full-length window overlooking the downtown skyline. This was during the streaker craze, and, sure enough, a stark naked man went jogging past the women. According to Pat Cremin, his cousin Billie Cremin-Smith glanced up, surveyed the situation, and went back to her game unperturbed.

"I didn't get a good look at his face," she said later, "but I saw enough to know that wasn't my husband."

Roy Clark had been sponsoring a celebrity golf tournament in Tulsa for years when someone approached him in early 1984 about lending his name to something called the Senior Tour. Clark's tournament would still benefit the Children's Medical Center, a charity for which he'd raised almost $800,000 over the years, but would be a regular PGA event—Tulsa's first ever.

Tulsa had been host to the PGA Championship, and the PGA sanctioned several Oklahoma Opens in the 1920s, but the city had never had a regular tour event. The Senior Tour, started in 1981 for touring veterans fifty years old and older, seemed a good way to get on the map—especially for Tulsa Country Club. The TCC course was too short for the regular tour but a perfect fit for the older guys.

PGA of America executive director Lou King, a former University of Tulsa football player whose wife Eunice was a Tulsa native, helped put the deal together on short notice. The sponsors and the club were eager to make the tournament work, even though the dates—June 14–17—were the same week as the U.S. Open as well as the state men's amateur.

The club had only four months to prepare—and, as it turned out, only a few days to do almost everything all over again.

Rain began falling the afternoon of May 26, 1984, a Saturday and the first day of the Memorial Day weekend. By Sunday morning, Tulsa had been inundated with a foot or more of rain and large sections of the city were flooded. Fourteen people would die in the Memorial Day Weekend flood of 1984, and property losses would approach $200 million.

Among the lesser casualties was Tulsa Country Club's carefully groomed golf course.

"It wiped us out," recalled Harold Neal, the TCC grounds superintendent at the time.

"All the sand was washed out of the sand traps," said Neal. "There were fish in the trap back of the sixth hole, and the bridge there had floated around to the No. 6 tee box."

According to accounts at the time, one hundred tons of sand had to be hauled onto the course to rebuild the bunkers.

"The heavy rains [that] produced flooding in Tulsa last weekend did not spare the TCC course," said the *Tulsa World* of June 3. "But the course was very much playable by midweek when a media group was given a tour."

The old pros themselves were quite complimentary when they arrived a week later.

Billy Casper was among the headliners in the 1984 Roy Clark Senior Challenge.

"The course is so good you wouldn't have known they had any floods," Don January, the Senior Tour's top money winner, told the *World*'s Clay Henry. "I've seen what water can do to golf courses. You wouldn't know it here."

The Senior Tour was proving popular with fans and the pros alike. Orville Moody, the 1969 U.S. Open champion, told Henry he happily joined the tour because "I need the money."

Billy Casper, the second golfer to reach $1 million in career earnings, pointed out he made $26,000 for winning the 1966 U.S. Open, while first-place money at the Roy Clark tournament was $30,000.

"I never dreamed [the Senior Tour] would grow this fast," Casper told *World* sports editor Bill Connors. "There are fellows out here who make more on the Senior Tour than they did on the regular tour."

First-round leader Art Silvestrone was a good example. A club pro from New Jersey, retired and

Oklahoman Orville Moody was another star of the Roy Clark Senior Challenge.

living in Florida, Silvestrone never played a full season on the regular tour and rated back-to-back New Jersey Open titles as the biggest victories of his career. But there he was, shooting an opening-round 68 to lead Moody and Dan Sykes by a shot.

Sykes, though, thought "anyone outside the top five players winning this week [would be] an upset. The better players will come to the front on a course like this."

Ten players were within three shots of the lead by the end of the second round. Silvestrone, January, and Sykes were tied at the top with one-under 141s. January fussed about his putting and said he couldn't get the hang of TCC's Bermuda grass fairways, but managed an even-par 71. Silvestrone stayed in contention with what he called a "halfway decent" 73. Sykes rallied for a 33 on the back nine and would have taken the lead had he not three-putted No. 18.

The third and last round provided an entertaining finish as Miller Barber birdied two of the last three holes—after saving par on No. 15—to beat January and Peter Thomson by a shot. Barber, with a 68, and Thomson, at 69, were the only players to break par on a day when the Oklahoma winds gusted to twenty-five miles an hour and several players, including Barber and January, were worried about making their flights.

Barber became known as "Mr. X" during his days on the regular tour because of his tendency to disappear between sunset and the next morning's tee time. On that last day in Tulsa, Barber again showed up just in time, shooting a 32 on the back nine with four birdies and a bogey. His best shot, though, may have been the one that rescued him from the bunker on No. 15 and left him a twelve-foot par putt. Barber didn't know it at the time, but the putt put him in a five-way tie for the lead.

Barber birdied Nos. 16 and 18, and then watched as January missed a four-foot putt on the last hole that would have forced a playoff.

The Roy Clark was one of twenty-five senior titles, including three U.S. Senior Opens, for Miller Barber.

"I played crappy," January growled to the *Tribune*'s Richard Linihan afterward. "I was choking my butt off, is what I was doing.

"It makes me want to throw up."

Barber, understandably, was more sanguine.

"I decided to come out and let the hammer drop today," he told Clay Henry. "I'm really happy. I played well.

"I'll be back," he said. "This is a fine, fine course, one I'd like to play every week."

At the time, it looked as though he would have the chance. Sponsors and Tour officials were encouraged enough that Tulsa and TCC had already been given a date for 1985, in late August this time and well away from the majors.

But it was not to be. Although generally considered a success, the tournament had not produced the payoff to Children's Medical Center that previous events had. And, by 1984, Tulsa was well into the second year of the 1980s oil bust. The collapse of Oklahoma City's Penn Square Bank had triggered bank failures throughout Oklahoma, including Tulsa. Millionaires suddenly found themselves bankrupt.

Once again, country clubs would have to reinvent themselves.

The Whiskey Cup, featuring golf and a cookout, was a popular all-male event during the early 1980s.

Bailey Word, 1986 club president, took the helm during the depths of the era's energy bust.

A 1984 club championship patch.

A. B. Steen, 1982 club president.

Don January won twenty-three PGA Senior Tour (now Champions Tour) events but missed a putt on the final hole to finish second to Miller Barber in the 1984 Roy Clark Senior Challenge.

Nothing seems to beat TCC's plain old Bermuda grass for challenging play out of short rough. Players in the 1984 Roy Clark Senior Challenge wrestled with it, and so did the entrants in the U.S. Senior Women's Amateur nearly twenty-five years later.

The present ninth hole was added during the Jay Morrish–designed refurbishment of the 1980s. Other major changes included converting the tenth and eighteenth holes to par four, a new twelfth hole, and reworking the old twelfth hole into the current seventeenth. The pond and landscaping at the ninth hole were made possible through the generosity of member Tom Russell.

CHAPTER EIGHT

Staying the Course

Country clubs are like any other business. They have to be kept up-to-date to remain competitive. So it was that by the mid-1980s, Tulsa Country Club was again considering major renovations to both its clubhouse and its golf course.

By 1983, membership numbers were on the slide, and not just at TCC. Every country club in town was fighting for every potential member it could find. In the midst of this, TCC's leadership began laying the groundwork for a major capital improvement project—a redesign of several holes, the complete rebuilding of all eighteen greens, refurbishment of the swimming pool, and substantial improvements to the clubhouse. All told, the tab was going to run to something more than $750,000.

This was not a universally popular idea. The membership, in fact, voted the proposal down the first time it came before them. The board, though, authorized the rebuilding of four greens and four tee boxes anyway, as allowed under the club's bylaws. The pool was also renovated.

For the golf course work, the board hired Jack Nicklaus protégé Jay Morrish. Morrish had just left Nicklaus's organization and set up his own business in Broken Arrow. His instructions were to recapture the course's original Tillinghast flavor.

"Jay has been very firm in that," TCC head pro Dave Bryan told the *World*'s Clay Henry in August 1985. "He is a big Tillinghast fan. He is trying to restore the greens just how Mr. Tillinghast would like them."

Over the next several months, Morrish's crews rebuilt the second, fifth, six, and fifteenth greens and the third, fifth, sixth, and sixteenth tee boxes. When the holes were opened to play the following spring, the most notable changes were the substitution of grass bunkers for sand traps on sixteen and the addition of a "tongue"—a Tillinghast hallmark—on No. 2 green.

The changes seem to have been generally well received, but that didn't mean the membership was ready to plunk down the money needed to carry out the rest of the planned renovations. As it turned out, 1986 was one of the club's toughest years in a long, long time.

"As most of you know," President Bailey Word wrote to the membership in early 1987, "1986 was a difficult year. . . . With that history and with Tulsa's unsettled economy, we did not feel that it was prudent to recommend a budget for 1987 that projects a net increase in membership."

Expenses were cut and salaries frozen. Even then, Word said, "it was impossible to balance the budget," necessitating a five-dollar-a-month dues increase.

The club was able to do a few things in 1986. Most notably, it acquired five hundred trees from a bankrupt nursery and planted them as part of a plan, devised by landscape architect Randy Heckenkemper, that called for the eventual addition of twice that number. In September, the club's new entrance gate was finished.

The club actually made some money—almost $100,000—in 1987, and that December the board once again brought a capital improvement project to a vote of the general membership. It passed this time, but not without some bitter dissent. A number of members left the club over the decision. Four members and one former member sued the board of directors.

The work was expensive—$400,000 for the course, $350,000 for the clubhouse, and another $55,000 for the halfway house—and would keep members off their course for the better part of a year. But the people most familiar with the course and the club were certain that something really needed to be done to keep TCC from falling behind its competitors.

"Innovative people in the club could see we had to do something," said Harold Neal, the course superintendent from 1981 to 2001. "A lot of people said it was not a good time, and we lost some members because of it. But we got a lot of new members because we did."

"It certainly inconveniences the membership," said former golf professional Tim Leslie in a 2008 interview. "They can't play the course while it's being worked on. That's costly to the club.

"But improvements have to happen. It's just one of those things."

The project did not get off to a good start. Just a week after the 1987 vote, the worst ice storm in memory and one of the worst on record hit Tulsa, splintering trees and littering the grounds with debris. The effect on the actual work was minimal, but it did seem a bad omen.

Key features of the overhaul included creating the current par-three ninth hole, converting the tenth to a par four and the eighteenth from an easy par five to a challenging par four, and replacing the existing twelfth hole with a new par three that plays as the current seventeenth hole.

"Jay went far beyond the call of duty as far as his time, effort, and enthusiasm," Forrest Shoemaker Jr., then the club president, told Clay Henry in 1988. "I don't think there is any question that his great admiration for Tillinghast had a lot to do with that."

"I think of it as his course and hope people will think it's back the way he would want it to be," Morrish told Henry.

Some discontent remained, though, including among those who did not believe Morrish had really done much to revive the Tillinghast style. Just about everyone, though, agreed the course had been improved by the work.

David Thompson, the green chairman during the Morrish rebuild, recalled one irascible older member telling him, "Dave, I've seen a lot of change in my life, and I've been against every bit of it. I was against this, but now I have to tell you it was the best thing we ever did."

Another jarring note during these years, though it had not directly impacted the club, was the continued deterioration and final demise of the old clubhouse.

The old place had fallen on very hard times indeed. There had been some talk in the late 1960s of turning it into a neighborhood recreation center, but that had come to nothing. The Tulsa Park Board looked at buying the pool. Finally, in 1973, TCC sold the clubhouse to a couple who envisioned it as a ballroom. Later it became a treatment center for drug addicts and the mentally ill. By the early 1980s, the building was again vacant and on the market.

But the once grand neighborhood had long ago lost its shine. Houses had fallen into disrepair. The Osage Hills Apartments, a prime property when built after World War II, had essentially turned into a public housing project that spawned crime and vandalism and scared away prospective investors.

In 1984, the clubhouse came into the possession of Grace Tucker—or, as she was usually known, Mother Tucker—who operated a north side rescue mission called the House of Prayer. Mother Tucker was the last refuge for the flotsam of society, the people who seemed to have nowhere to go and no idea how to get there. By the time she moved into the old clubhouse, her charges included the increasing number of homeless mental patients being released from Eastern State Hospital in Vinita.

"I know this is not the right environment for them," Tucker said in a 1984 interview with the *World*'s Beth Macklin, "but nobody else wants them."

Their new haven did not last long. On Thanksgiving morning of 1986, the clubhouse's ancient wiring system short-circuited and the building went up in flames. Ultimately, sadly, the old girl had to be demolished.

The format of the Oklahoma Golf Association's state amateur championships has varied since the popularization of stroke play after World War II. In some years, it has decided the championship by match play, in others by stroke play. And, in some years, it has had both stroke-play and match-play champions. At the state amateur played at Tulsa Country Club in 1986, both a stroke-play and a match-play champion were crowned.

Tulsa Country Club's old clubhouse went up in flames on Thanksgiving morning 1986. It had been put to various uses, including a ballroom, before becoming a rescue mission operated by Grace "Mother" Tucker.

The stroke-play champion was Mike Hughett, a twenty-seven-year-old accountant, former Oral Roberts University golfer, and new Tulsa Country Club member. Hughett tore up the first round for a 68 and a six-shot lead, then shot a one-over 71 for the second round to win by eight shots.

A former Nebraska state champion, Hughett had finished his collegiate career at the University of Nebraska after starting at ORU and was largely unknown to the field he beat so handily. That would not be the case for long. Hughett and four-ball partner Eric Mueller soon established themselves as two of the most formidable players in the state.

The sixty-four-man stroke-play field included several other TCC notables, including Mueller, club president Bailey Word, and club champion Jim Unruh, at fifty-seven the only senior in the

tournament. TCC's scene-stealer, though, would turn out to be an employee rather than a member.

Hughett and Mueller both benefited from unusual circumstances in the second round. Mueller won his second-round match when his opponent locked his keys in his car and missed his tee time. Hughett received a third-round forfeit when Todd Baker of Tulsa beat Jim Hayes, also of Tulsa, 1-up in twenty-two holes in the second round, then announced he was withdrawing from the tournament to play in a benefit.

The free passes did not help Mueller or Hughett. Mueller lost in the next round to defending champion Fred Lutz of Oklahoma City. Twenty-year-old TCC pro shop employee Kyle Flinton beat Hughett in the quarterfinals.

Although not well known statewide, Flinton had won the city championship earlier that year and also an area amateur. He beat Jack Ingram of Tulsa 3-and-2 in the semifinals to reach the championship match against Bob Mase, a Tulsa landman and former University of Texas golfer.

Mase readily admitted to being as surprised as anyone to find himself in the final.

"Like everybody else out here who works for a living, I haven't had time to play enough," he told *The Oklahoman*'s Tom Kensler.

That caught up with Mase in the finals. Flinton birdied the second hole of the thirty-six-hole final and was 3-up after the morning round. He birdied two of the first three afternoon holes to go 5-up and shut off any attempt at a rally by Mase. The match ended after thirty holes with Flinton winning 8-and-6.

Saying he intended to turn pro two days later, Flinton told Kensler, "Not a bad way to end my amateur career."

Flinton, in fact, would go on to win three national PGA assistant club pro championships, and led the 2008 national PGA pro tournament through three rounds before finishing third. He is now head pro at Oklahoma City's Quail Creek Golf & Country Club.

Bob Mase, the workingman's golfer, kept plugging away, too. In 1997, at the Golf Club of Oklahoma, he finally won a state amateur title.

TCC members Eric Mueller, left, and Mike Hughett became one of the Tulsa area's best four-ball teams during the late 1980s and early 1990s. Between them, they accounted for nine straight club championships, and Hughett won a state amateur stroke-play championship.

President Rex J. Williams surveyed the damage of "a turbulent year" in the club's 1988 annual report.

"We weathered a considerable reduction in our membership," he wrote, "due in part to resignations by members who opposed the improvement program."

The oil bust, though, was the biggest culprit. Oklahoma's economy in the mid-1980s was five times more dependent on energy than the nation's as a whole. As oil tumbled from forty dollars a barrel to ten, it took with it almost a quarter of the state's banks and exacerbated the local effects of a national real estate mortgage crisis. In 1989 the Resolution Trust Corporation, the federal entity set up to dispose of failed savings and loan assets, moved into the downtown building once owned by Samuel Grant Kennedy and his family. Over the next three years, Tulsa's RTC office would dispose of nearly $6 billion worth of foreclosed property in Oklahoma and Arkansas.

It's no surprise, then, that Tulsa Country Club's revenues dropped 15 percent from 1987 to 1988, or that stockholding membership numbered only 347 in 1990. In early 1992, the *Tulsa Tribune*—itself soon to disappear from the city's landscape—reported a "buyers' market" for country club memberships. The Golf Club of Oklahoma had waived its $40,000 buy-in for more than a hundred new members. Cedar Ridge cut its initiation fee from $16,000 to $12,500. TCC memberships, the newspaper said, were going for $3,000. In July, it was announced the club had lost $50,000 through the first six months of 1992.

In its effort to tap unexplored revenue sources, the club started offering yoga classes and tips on exercise and flexibility. It hosted business seminars, and for a number of years was the site of an annual University of Tulsa energy and environmental symposium.

By 1993, the worst was over. Cleve Stubblefield arrived that year as club manager and remembers, "When I got there, it was kind of after the hit. We started rebuilding."

One immediate obstacle, though, was a change in federal tax laws. At the behest of the new Clinton administration and with Vice President Al Gore casting the deciding vote in the Senate, Congress eliminated the long-standing business exemption for country club dues and reduced the deduction for meals and entertainment from 80 percent to 50 percent.

Needless to say, this was not popular with country clubs or their members—so much so that Gore's request to play Tulsa Country Club while in town for the Democratic Governors Conference during the summer of 1993 was turned down.

"Most of the other clubs in town are near where people live," Stubblefield said in a 1993 *Tulsa World* interview. "We are near where people work. We have a lot of members who conduct business on the golf course as well as in the clubhouse. I don't see us losing a lot of members, but I can see a lot of people backing off and not spending as much . . .

until they see how the new laws really affect them."

Now general manager of Cedar Ridge Country Club, Stubblefield says in retrospect the biggest impact may have been on people and corporations holding memberships in more than one club.

"At that time, a lot of people belonged to more than one club," he said. "And not just in Tulsa. They may have one in Tulsa and one in, say, Phoenix. A lot of them decided not to do that any more, and we lost some members that way."

But, for the most part, Tulsa Country Club members are a hardy lot. Stubblefield said his fondest memories of the club are from time spent with the likes of F. Lee Murdock, who had been the club president in the 1950s and before that, as greens chairman, arranged the exhibitions with Sam Sneed and Byron Nelson.

"He was kind of a grumpy old man by that time, to be honest," Stubblefield said. "But if he said 'Hello' to me, I knew he was in the mood

Vice President Al Gore was denied permission to play golf at TCC shortly after casting the deciding vote for a tax bill detrimental to country clubs.

to talk. He was a country club guy. He knew everything and everybody."

Race became a national issue for country clubs in the summer of 1990. Hall Thompson, the founder of an Alabama club scheduled to host that year's PGA championship, created a stir by saying blacks were excluded from membership. This led to a round of self-examination in Tulsa, where it was concluded that while very few blacks belonged to area country clubs, none in recent memory had been excluded by race.

Tulsa Country Club, as it turned out, had been integrated some years earlier not by a captain of industry or leader of the community, but by a small girl.

Her name was Catherine, and she was the adopted daughter of Pat and Margie Cremin. Pat remembers calling David Thompson to tell him their daughter was African American and Cremin was ready to put up a fight for her if necessary. Thompson laughed.

"You think we care?" he said.

"Our daughter just loved it," Cremin said of her childhood at the club. "She practically lived at the pool. And nobody ever said anything unpleasant to her; she was part of the group. It was a big help."

The little girl grew, got married, started a family of her own.

"Now her daughter is a regular here also," said Cremin.

Okmulgee's Joe Nick was hot when he came to the OGA stroke play championship at Tulsa Country Club in July 1993. He had won five association events in a row and was the odds-on favorite to make the stroke play title his sixth.

Nick's strategy was simple: Dr. Pepper and little chocolate doughnuts.

That's what he had every morning before teeing off. It had been working pretty well, even if his swing didn't look like much.

"Joe is one of those guys that's not real pretty," said Eric Mueller, who had lost to Nick in the finals of the 1992 match play tournament, in a pre-tournament interview with the *World*'s Dan O'Kane. "You watch his setup and swing and you don't think he's that good a player, but he's a great one."

But Nick could not keep up with Oklahoma City's Tim Graves, who shot a 68 on the first day and a 71 on the second to lead by five strokes going into the final round. He was cruising along with a six-shot lead with six holes to play when he clanked his tee shot off a tree on thirteen and then missed a three-foot putt to double-bogey the hole.

Graves three-putted the fourteenth and bogeyed seventeen when his two-foot birdie putt hit a spike mark. When he bogeyed eighteen, Graves found himself in a tie with Pryor's Gary Gowan.

Graves had lost the year's match play championship to Nick in similar fashion and could feel this one slipping away, too. This time, though, he gathered himself and played No. 1—the first playoff hole—with antiseptic precision, ending with a two-foot par putt and the championship.

And Nick? Well, he shot 78 on the last day and faded to fifteenth.

So much for Dr. Pepper and little chocolate doughnuts.

Tillinghouse—the new halfway house overlooking the pond on the sixth hole—was finished in 1995. It was the last piece of the capital improvement package approved eight years earlier. They had been difficult years but also rewarding. Once again, the club was prospering.

And, it was about to embark on one of the busiest periods of its nearly one hundred-year existence.

Tillinghouse, the snack bar overlooking the water on the sixth hole, was completed in 1996.

*Course architect A. W. Tillinghast still looks over the course,
in the form of this statue just east of the present clubhouse.
After years of obscurity, Tillinghast's courses are again in favor.*

CHAPTER NINE

Tillie's Ghost

A. W. Tillinghast believed golf should be played more with brains than brawn, that precision should trump power, and that the best golf courses presented a challenging yet fair test to players of widely varying ability.

"We regard the present tendency to stretch courses out to greater lengths than ever before as an unfortunate and mistaken policy," he wrote long before graphite shafts and urethane balls. "To make our courses more enjoyable to the great majority, we rather incline to the conviction that shorter holes and smaller greens would be much better."

For all its changes over the years, the Tulsa Country Club course has remained true to that precept. As championship courses have grown to ever-greater dimensions, TCC has remained within its bounds. To be sure, it has had little opportunity to expand, surrounded as it is by residential neighborhoods and given the prohibitive costs of course construction. But the course has not been tricked up, either. It retains the subtle integrity of a Tillinghast design.

"A lot of people have never figured out this golf course," said Don Eustice, who first played it as a boy in the 1930s. "People look at it, think 'I'll just kill it,' but they never do. Every hole has a place that's hard to get out of."

"When Morrish was working here," Forrest Shoemaker Jr. said in 2008, "I can remember him saying this course was good enough that by toughening it up, you could make it good enough to play a major on. I'm not sure that's still the case, because now the courses have to be longer. But I've played all the courses in Tulsa, and none of them has anything on this one except length."

The club's commitment, through good times and bad, to maintain this basic concept—and its long association with the University of Tulsa's women's golf program—paid off during the 1990s when a succession of tournaments brought TCC national attention and put Tulsa on the Ladies Professional Golf Association Tour.

TU had no women's golf before Dale McNamara and virtually no women's athletic program of any kind. As a student in the late 1950s, McNamara was presented an honorary letter by the athletic department for the golf tournaments she was winning without any help from the university. In 1974, when McNamara volunteered to coach a golf team that existed only on paper, she had a budget of $1,500 and no players. McNamara recruited her first team on campus. Her second team included a shy freshman named Nancy Lopez and finished second in the nation.

Tulsa Country Club had long enjoyed a relationship with the TU men's golf program. That soon extended to the fledgling women's program. The teams practiced on the TCC course and frequently hosted tournaments there. By the late 1980s, an annual collegiate tournament was drawing some of the best teams in the country to the club.

McNamara won four national championships from 1980 to 1988 and finished second five times in her twenty-six years leading the program. She

Among the physical changes to the club during the 1990s was a deck overlooking the first tee and the downtown skyline.

coached eighteen All-Americans and sent a dozen or more players to the pro tour, including Lopez, Jody Rosenthal Anschutz, Kathy Baker Guadagnino, Cathy Reynolds, Carolyn Hill, Kelly Robbins, and Stacy Prammanasudh. But, as McNamara entered her third decade of coaching, she had one more goal to accomplish—bring the NCAA women's championship tournament to Tulsa.

McNamara and TU made a formal pitch to Tulsa Country Club in November 1996. The club quickly agreed. It had successfully held the 1994 National Association of Intercollegiate Athletic tournament, was scheduled for the 1997 tournament, and was making a determined effort to land more high-profile events. In August 1997, McNamara and TCC announced they had been awarded the 1999 Division I championship.

"With the tremendous success that past amateur and professional tournaments have enjoyed in Tulsa, combined with the national and international exposure that TU women's golf has brought to this community, it seems only fitting that the city of Tulsa, TU, and TCC host this event," TCC president Mike Perry told the *Tulsa World*.

McNamara was ecstatic.

"This means so much to me," she said. "I get emotional just thinking about it."

It could be argued that the run-up to the NCAA championship actually started in the summer of 1996, when the Women's Oklahoma Golf Association state amateur came to Tulsa Country Club. The field included several fine collegiate players, including the University of Oklahoma's Kim McFarlin and Megan Waller and the University of New Mexico's Megan Benn and Angie Hopkins.

McFarlin was the qualifying medalist, and Benn and Hopkins reached the semifinals, but the winner was Oklahoma State University assistant coach Sheila Luginbuel Dills. Dills dominated match play, beating Benn 5-and-4 in the final to win her third straight state amateur and fourth overall.

But nothing in Tulsa Country Club's history required quite the commitment the NCAA championship did. McNamara was not kidding around when she said, "I know how huge an undertaking this will be."

TU and TCC hadn't just signed up for one major event. They had signed up for three: the championship itself, a preview tournament seven months ahead of the championship, and, ultimately, a pro-am to pay for the other two.

Sponsored by Williams and played in late August 1998, the pro-am featured some of McNamara's most prized pupils, including her daughter Melissa as well as Anschutz, Guadagnino, Hill, Cathy Mockett, Adele Lukken-Peterson, and Barb Whitehead. Lukken-Peterson, a Tulsa native playing with her father Robert and three others, won the pro-am, but the importance of the tournament was the impression it made on the visiting pros. Most of them stayed at the Williams Companies' lodge in the hills northwest of town.

All said they had a good time.

"I think all of us have been bugging Dale for a long time to have one of these," Anschutz told the *Tulsa World*.

"We told her if she'd get something here, we'd all come back and we'd bring a few friends. I think this has been a huge success. It was definitely a lot of fun for the pros."

Besides raising money for the collegiate tournaments, the pro-am had been something of a tryout for the LPGA Tour. TCC and Tulsa passed with high marks.

"The success of Monday's event," wrote *Tulsa World* sports columnist John Klein, "leads to speculation that more will follow. Virtually all of the players said Tulsa would be a great place for a regular LPGA Tour stop."

The Fall Preview was played the first week of October. Eighteen of the nation's top teams comprised the field. Individual stars included Duke's Jenny Chuasiripron, who had lost the U.S. Open in a playoff, and Arizona State's Grace Park, the 1998 U.S. Amateur and Trans-National winner. Also in the tournament were defending NCAA champion Jennifer Rosales of Southern California and the nation's top junior, Duke freshman Beth Bauer.

Seven inches of rain washed out the tournament's first round and left the greens soft when play did begin. Led by even-par 71s from Chuasiripron and Bauer, Duke slogged to a 13-over 297 and a three-shot lead on USC. Tulsa, Oklahoma State, and Arizona State were four shots back. TU's Niina Laitinen and freshman Stacy Prammanasudh, who had won the All-State high school girls' title on the TCC course just a few months earlier, each had a 73.

Laitinen charged to the front on the final round, shooting a 71 that included a shot out of the woods on No. 3—her last hole from a shotgun start—that caromed off a photographer and landed just behind the green. Laitinen pitched to within four feet of the hole and putted out to save par and medalist honors.

The eighteen teams combined to shoot sixty-nine strokes higher than the previous day, and Duke held on to win the team title by two shots over TU and four over USC.

"I think this course just wears you out," OSU coach Ann Pitts told the *World*. "There are no holes where you can make a quick recovery from a previous mistake. It just gets more difficult as you go along."

Chuasiripron predicted better scores once the championships came around.

"The course will probably be drier and play shorter," she said. "And we should all be on top of our games by the end of spring."

If only she had known.

Playing conditions were almost perfect for the first round of the women's championship on May 19, 1999. The temperature topped out at eighty degrees. Skies were clear. Oklahoma's notorious spring wind was hardly more than a whisper.

And still Terrible Tillie wreaked his revenge.

Only Duke, at 288, broke 300. Park, at 69, was the only player to beat par. The average round for the day was 78.1.

"I am a little surprised by the scores," Park told the *World*'s Dan O'Kane. "This golf course is tough, but to be honest it's not that tough."

Others said more or less the same thing—until the next day, when variable winds gusted to twenty-three miles per hour and the threat of lightning suspended play for nearly two hours. Birdies remained hard to come by, and players and coaches began to grudgingly admit there was more to the TCC course than immediately met the eye.

"It's probably something about this golf course [and] the way it is set up," Arizona State coach Linda Vollstedt suggested to the *World*'s Bill Haisten. "When you see really good players with some of these scores, then you know it is a little more challenging than most."

One team that did improve was Tulsa. After a near-disaster in the first round, the Golden Hurricane shot a 300 on the second day to move from thirteenth to ninth. Filippa Helmersson, practically in tears after a first-round 83, recovered to shoot 72 on the second day to lead TU.

The third round presented yet another set of circumstances. An early-morning rain softened the greens and calmed the wind, yet scores went still higher. Duke remained the team leader, eight strokes ahead of Georgia and defending champion Arizona State. Park eagled the par-five fifth hole—her seventh from the shotgun start—to regain the individual lead by a stroke over Duke's Candy Hannemann.

TU matched its second-round 300 and moved up to sixth.

The final day of the tournament was notable because it didn't happen. Not officially. Even though Arizona State caught Duke at the turn and Park and Hannemann were still locked in a duel through eleven, the record book shows it never happened.

A storm—a doozy even by Oklahoma standards—blew in at four in the afternoon with the last players on the back nine. The billowing blue-green clouds packed eighty-mile-per-hour winds and four-inch hail. Many of the players had never seen Mother Nature in such a conniption; some, fascinated by the spectacle, pressed so hard against the clubhouse's full-length windows it was feared they might push the glass from its frame.

By the time the storm passed, it was too late to finish the round. And, in any event, it is doubtful the course could have been made ready to play.

For just about any other event, the situation would have caused a delay until the next day or until conditions permitted. Not by the rules of the NCAA women's golf championship. The next day was Sunday, and a rule instituted for two schools not even in the tournament prohibited play on Sunday. It did not allow suspension of play or postponement. The championship was to be decided based on the three completed rounds. Duke was declared team champion, Park the individual medalist.

So it was that the 1999 NCAA golf championship at Tulsa Country Club led to a rules change. From that day on, every national tournament has included a rain day.

Arizona State's Grace Park was medalist in the rain-shortened 1999 NCAA Division I women's championship at Tulsa Country Club.

Head golf professional Jeff Combe joined the club staff in 1990 and became head pro in 1992. A former All-American at Oral Roberts University, he was one of the region's best playing professionals during the 1990s.

In its early days, the LPGA was a frequent visitor to Oklahoma, with tour stops in Lawton, Burneyville, Ardmore, and Muskogee. Muskogee Country Club was the site of the U.S. Golf Association's 1970 Women's Open.

The LPGA, in fact, had strong connections to the central United States. It had been formed at a meeting during the U.S. Women's Open in Wichita in 1950, and most of the thirteen founding members were from the middle tier of states. The most prominent of them, Babe Didrikson Zaharias, was a Texan. So was tiny Bettye Danoff. Another, Betty Jameson, was a native of Norman who attended the University of Texas. Marilynn Smith was from Topeka, Kansas, and Opal Hill was from Kansas City. Sisters Alice Bauer and Marlene Hagge were from South Dakota. Betsy Rawls, a Phi Beta Kappa graduate of the University of Texas, was one of the LPGA's first stars.

McNamara played as an amateur in some of those early LPGA tournaments in Oklahoma.

"I used to go around with the pros and help set up the courses," she said in a 1998 story by O'Kane. "The LPGA was in its very beginning days. It was fascinating. It was just a caravan of tournaments."

By the 1970s, though, the LPGA was gravitating toward the West Coast and the South; by the mid-1980s, it had no regular tour stop between St. Louis and Phoenix. McNamara and others in Tulsa set about to rectify the situation.

The 1998 Williams LPGA Pro-Am, originally scheduled as a fundraiser for that year's collegiate Fall Classic, became the catalyst.

"We housed the players up at the lodge, and we had the most wonderful pro-am," McNamara said in 2008. "The LPGA fell in love with Tulsa and with the course. And that was the beginning of the LPGA's interest in Tulsa."

Keith Bailey, then the head of Williams Companies, became an important proponent of bringing the LPGA to Tulsa.

"He asked a lot of the LPGA players what they thought about coming here," recalled Tulsa Country

Club head golf professional Jeff Combe in 2008. "They all said the city was wonderful and the course was spectacular to play."

Just a few days after the NCAA championships in 1999, the *Tulsa World* reported that the LPGA hoped to have a tournament at Tulsa Country Club the next year, although club officials doubted it could be arranged that soon.

"We don't know if that gives us enough time," Stubblefield told O'Kane. "It looks like it could happen the first or second week of September 2001."

The key individuals were Bailey, TCC greens chairman and Williams executive Bill Von Glahn, Combe, Stubblefield, TCC directors, McNamara, and McNamara's daughter Melissa, who represented Williams on the LPGA tour and was a member of the tour's executive committee.

Finally, in November 2000, a tour official confirmed that the $1 million Williams LPGA Championship was scheduled for the following September at Tulsa Country Club, and that it would be one of only three LPGA tournaments with full-field network television coverage.

It was, as O'Kane pointed out in early 2001, going to be a busy year for golf in Oklahoma. Besides the Williams Championship, the U.S. Open was scheduled for June 14–17 at Southern Hills and the Senior PGA Tour Championship was to be played in early August at Gaillardia Golf and Country Club in Oklahoma City.

Some thought the U.S. Open might cut into the Williams Championship, but LPGA officials disagreed and in the end they were right. The tournament was a hit.

But there were some scary moments. A tough winter killed off a disturbing amount of fairway grass. In April, the practice green turned a sickly yellow; within two weeks, the rest of the putting surfaces were similarly peaked in appearance. The malady, ultimately diagnosed as pythium root rot, was treated, and by mid-May the greens were, well, green again—but not before considerable

Annika Sorenstam became an early supporter of the Williams LPGA. She won the 2002 championship.

anxiety on the part of the TCC membership. Recriminations were such that when Harold Neal, the club's superintendent of twenty years, resigned shortly after to enter the irrigation business, word got around that he had been forced out. The rumor wasn't true, but it was an indication of how important the approaching tournament was to the members—and a reminder of how difficult a course superintendent's job can be.

The summer was unusually hot and dry, even for Oklahoma, and the course went three months without rain. At its hottest in July, the club was putting a half-million gallons of water a day on the course, which made for some breathtaking water bills but kept the course in fighting trim. As late as mid-August, volunteer member work crews—armed with ample supplies of cold liquid refreshment—were on the course fixing divots and pulling weeds.

It all paid off in September. The weather broke, and Stubblefield declared the course up to the job. The greens, he told Bill Haisten, "were the worst going into the spring that they've been in a long time, and now our fairways and greens are in the best shape at this time of year that they've ever been."

Besides Williams, the tournament had sixty-five sponsors at levels from $1,000 to $100,000. A week out, advance ticket sales were approaching tour officials' projected totals for the entire event.

Activities actually began on Monday, September 3, with a qualifying round for the last two spots in the field of 144. Practice rounds were played on Tuesday, as was a four-hole alternate-shot "shootout" featuring Nancy Lopez, Melissa McNamara, Jan Stephenson, Wendy Ward, Nancy Scranton, and five local amateurs.

A regular pro-am was played on Wednesday and Thursday, with the fifty-four-hole Williams LPGA Championship Friday through Sunday.

The field included most of the tour's biggest stars, including Annika Sorenstam, Karrie Webb, and the semiretired Lopez, who had not played a competitive round of golf in Tulsa since leaving TU in 1977. Stacy Prammanasudh, now a TU All-American, was entered as an amateur using a sponsor exemption.

More than eleven thousand spectators—about 40 percent more than expected—showed up for Friday's opening round. The wind was ferocious, gusting to more than forty miles per hour in the afternoon. It became so bad the hand-held scoreboards following the players had to be brought in because the removable letters and numerals were flying all over the course.

Angie Ridgeway, after shooting a 75, sighed to reporters, "We've played in some strong wind this year, but I don't remember it being this gusty. My head hurts. I shot five over. I worked my butt off for five-over."

TU ex Kelly Robbins shot a two-under 68 and said, "I'm glad that's over."

Robbins and Gloria Park led after the first day. Susie Redman and Rachel Teske were a shot back.

Lopez, not surprisingly, drew a large gallery but did not play particularly well, shooting a twelve-over 82. Prammanasudh struggled to a 76. Sorenstam shot a 72, Webb a 74; neither was ever a factor in the tournament.

Hall of Famer Nancy Lopez played on the TCC course as an All-American at the University of Tulsa. She returned in 2001 to help launch the Williams LPGA Championship.

University of Tulsa product Stacy Prammanasudh from the eighteenth tee during the first Williams LPGA Challenge in September 2001.

The second day belonged to Donna Andrews. The thirty-four-year-old Virginian had not won on tour since falling off a horse two years earlier, but with the wind dying down and the day cooler, Andrews tamed the TCC layout like no one ever had. She shot a 62, two strokes better than Combe's men's course record and six better than the women's record. She would have had a 61, but assessed herself a one-stroke penalty on eighteen for supposedly hitting a putt twice—although no one saw it and even Andrews wasn't sure.

"I have to go by what I felt," she told Haisten, "and I felt like the putter slowed down and I nicked it a second time. They call this a gentlemen's game, or whatever, and with this you have to go with your gut instinct."

But Andrews's round wasn't the only good one on Saturday. Karen Weiss, who had a 76 for the first round, shot 64 for the second. Teske had a 67, Ward a 66, and Rosie Jones a 65. Teske, Ward, and Jones all trailed Andrews by four shots going into the final round. Five other players were within six shots.

Andrews said several players were capable of catching her, and she was right. When she bogeyed the third hole—statistically the easiest hole on the course—the race was on. Five players were within two shots after six holes, and by the time Andrews made the turn she trailed Gloria Park by a shot.

Teske, Ward, and Jones fell out of contention, but Andrews and Park remained neck-and-neck.

Andrews got back even, but Park birdied seventeen to regain the lead. Playing a hole behind Park, Andrews needed a birdie on eighteen to tie. She reached the green—barely—in two, but rolled a thirty-five-foot putt just wide of the cup.

Park, a twenty-one-year-old South Korean who'd never finished better than ninth in an LPGA tournament, had won by one stroke—the stroke Andrews had penalized herself the day before.

Despite the outbreak of birdies on Saturday, Park was the only player with three below-par rounds. She finished with an eight-under 201 total. Teske managed a 71 on the final day and finished six shots back at 207.

"I didn't let my emotions get to me," Park told reporters. "I didn't let a bad shot on one hole turn into bad shots on two holes. I went to the next hole and hit my normal shots."

Andrews offered her own rendition of the golfers' lament.

"Even my good shots didn't turn out good today," she told the *World*'s John Hoover. "That's the difference. Yesterday even the bad shots turned out good.

"I made million miles of putts yesterday," Andrews continued. "Today, I couldn't get them to the hole."

Tournament organizers seemed pleased. Financial and attendance goals were met and exceeded. Players seemed happy. Perfect weather on the final day brought out 18,000 spectators, putting the total for the week over 56,000.

"There was never any doubt in my mind how this city would receive this tournament," said Dale McNamara. "I know what a wonderful golf city this is. I know what kind of community spirit we have here."

The glow did not last long. McNamara's remarks appeared in Klein's column on the morning of September 11, 2001—the morning terrorists flew jetliners into New York's World Trade Center and the Pentagon.

Former TU golfer Kelly Robbins, right, and Karrie Webb on the sixth hole during a practice round for the 2001 Williams LPGA Championship.

Sheila Dills won the 1996 Oklahoma State amateur at TCC.

CHAPTER TEN

Second Century

he NCAA and LPGA tournaments raised Tulsa Country Club's visibility and its expectations to new heights. Its name and its panoramic view of Tulsa's skyline had become familiar to millions of television viewers. Its course and reputation for hospitality were now well known among some of the country's top golfers. The LPGA tour players voted the first Williams Championship the best stop of 2001.

Such events can be a lot of work—not to mention inconvenience—but the majority of members seemed happy for the attention and the accolades. Williams, the LPGA, and the club had a three-year agreement, but after the 2001 tournament, there was much reason to believe Tulsa Country Club would continue to be the site of a major women's tournament well beyond that.

Fate and circumstances intervened.

No matter how hard it tries, Tulsa has never been able to pull completely free of the energy market's elliptical orbit. At least as far back as 1907, when a local newspaper reporter suggested Tulsa reposition itself as the "asparagus capital of the world," it has diligently sought to diversify its economic base.

And to a large extent, it has. Although asparagus never made it big here, aerospace and telecommunications have. Unfortunately for Tulsa, by early 2002, aerospace, telecommunications, and energy were all three in trouble—and Williams was a major player in two of them. Shares in Williams's communications subsidiary fell from a high of sixty-one dollars to sixty-seven cents at the end of 2001. Then, in early 2002, Williams revealed that it stood to lose up to $100 million from the collapse of energy giant Enron.

Despite its troubles, Williams stuck by its commitment to the LPGA. Technically, Williams did not merely sponsor the tournament. It owned it. But given the company's precarious situation, no one could have criticized it for simply walking away. That's what other sponsors were doing. Abrupt withdrawals, in fact, had left the LPGA without a Florida tournament for the first time ever.

As the second Williams Championship approached in September 2002, though, the company's director of marketing, Fran Evans, said event revenues were almost $1 million ahead of the previous year at the same point.

"Right now," Evans told the *Tulsa World*, "our plan is to be here in 2003."

The course, at least, was in outstanding condition. The winter had been milder and the summer wetter and not as hot as the previous year, so the fairways were lush and deep and the greens short and fast. Twelve tee-boxes had been reworked and the outline of an old creek bed in front of the thirteenth green deepened enough to hold water. Superintendent Tim Lampton confidently predicted there would be no repeat of Donna Andrews's 62.

The field included Andrews, defending champion Gloria Park, Juli Inkster, and the top two players on the LPGA money list, Annika Sorenstam and Se Ri Pak. The first-round leader, though, was Tracy Hanson, who shot a six-under 64 to lead seventeen players under par on a stifling ninety-seven-degree day.

Sorenstam surged to the front in round two, shooting a 66 for a six-under 134 total. Veteran Lorie Kane, who had entered the tournament on Sorenstam's recommendation, shot a 64 and was one shot back. Twenty-two other players were within six strokes of the lead.

"Tomorrow is the day that counts," said Sorenstam. "I'm going to keep being aggressive and not worry too much about the other players."

Indeed, she had little reason to. With almost 21,000 spectators turning out for the final round on a perfect September afternoon, Sorenstam birdied four of the last six holes for a 65 and beat Kane by four shots. The $150,000 first prize pushed Sorenstam over $2 million in earnings for the second straight year. It was her thirty-eighth career victory.

"I bogeyed the first hole and my caddie said, 'It's okay. We've got seventeen more to go. Just keep playing,'" she told the *World*. "I made some great putts when I needed to, so it was a good day, definitely."

The following April, Williams assigned its sponsorship to sports management and marketing firm Octagon but agreed to fulfill its $2 million obligation to the 2003 tournament. Three months later, hotelier John Q. Hammons assumed title sponsorship. It was a good deal for the LPGA and for Tulsa, but it did not bode well for Tulsa Country Club's continued involvement in the event. Hammons had just opened a new hotel in far southeast Tulsa, making a change of venue for the tournament almost certain.

Nevertheless, the 2003 tournament went off with the same precision as its predecessors, despite nine inches of rain early in the week. The field included Sorenstam, the defending champion, and Karrie Webb, stuck in the longest winless streak of her storied career.

Webb got off to a good start, though, posting a five-under 65 for a first-day one-shot lead on Donna Andrews and two on Tammie Green.

Sorenstam, playing for the first time in three weeks, struggled to a 72.

With the greens noticeably drier, faster, and more unpredictable, only nine players beat par on Saturday's second round. Webb was one of them. Her 69 put her three shots up on

Karrie Webb won the 2003 John Q. Hammons championship, the last of the three LPGA events played at Tulsa Country Club in the early 2000s.

Recent improvements have included a $1.5 million renovation of the pool and pool area, including slides, water features, a lounge, and outdoor dining decks.

Christie Kerr and four on Andrews and University of Tulsa product Stacy Prammanasudh.

"It was really hard to determine how the ball was going to react hitting the green," Webb told *World* reporter Matt Doyle. "It was sort of a guessing game."

The twenty-nine-year-old Australian continued to guess better than anyone else. Her third-round 66 put her ten under for the tournament and gave her a nine-shot victory over Dorothy Delasin, Candie Kung, Jamie Hullett, and Tammie Green. It was Webb's first victory in twenty-three tournaments, dating back to 2002.

"I'm really happy and a little relieved to play really well today," Webb told Doyle. "It's not so much winning by nine, but just that I played well enough to win. It's just a sense of relief, and I'm proud because it's not been the easiest of years for me."

The tournament ended on September 7. The announcement that it was moving to Cedar Ridge, just down the road from Hammons's new hotel, came eight days later. Tim Erensen, the tournament's executive director, told the *World* that the change was "a 100 percent business decision for Mr. Hammons."

TCC members understood. They understood—but that didn't mean they liked it. The previous six years had awakened the club to its possibilities, and with its centennial approaching, there was not much sentiment for fading quietly into the background. Soon after the LPGA move to Cedar Ridge became official, Tulsa Country Club began casting around for other means to showcase itself.

"When the LPGA tournament left, a lot of members involved with it got together," Jeff Combe said in 2008. "They wanted to continue pursuing other events. That's when we got involved with the USGA."

In late April 2004, USGA officials visited Tulsa Country Club for talks about hosting an event. Initially, the most likely appeared to be the Girls Junior Championship.

"The Girls Junior Championship is a good match for us," club president Steve Stecher told the *World*'s Dan O'Kane. "We have experience hosting women's events. [The course] sets up well for them, and the membership enjoys it."

O'Kane reported that TCC had informed the USGA it would take anything that came open, even stepping in if another host club dropped out. The goal, O'Kane wrote, was to eventually land a U.S. Women's Open.

"The way the USGA works is that you have to prove yourself with a second tier championship," said Stecher. "Once you've proven yourself, then you can get in line for one of the bigger championships. The Women's Open is one that we can handle, and we would like to do it."

This was not an endeavor to be undertaken lightly. Even a second-tier USGA event means countless hours of work for staff and volunteers and a significant investment of resources. Immediate financial rewards are minimal at best. But the long-term benefits—tangible and intangible—can be enormous.

Golf was not the only matter of interest for Tulsa Country Club as its centennial year approached. Members were becoming increasingly value-conscious, demanding a wide range of services and activities, from dining to fitness facilities. A $1.5 million pool complex and grill were installed on the south end of the clubhouse. Additional training equipment was installed and courses in such regimens as yoga and Pilates offered.

"Younger members today don't see club membership as a symbol of social status," said club general manager Jason Fiscus. "When we're talking to prospective members, they have to be able to justify the expense of membership to their family. Many look at it as saving eighty dollars a month by dropping a health club membership."

"It used to be, you'd go to eat there on Friday night, and there would be three families," said longtime member Pat Cremin. "Now you have to have reservations. It's become a great dining facility—a Friday night destination.

"You also see now a consistent effort to entertain the kids. That's been a real emphasis. You see a lot more young families the last several years."

Fiscus said the average member age is forty-nine, ten years younger than the national average and "especially unusual for an older club like ours."

"We've made a conscious effort to target our services to families, and we've grown our membership considerably the last three years," he said.

Social memberships, Fiscus said, have jumped from 60 to about 150.

Among the activities are a monthly family night, featuring movies for the kids and dinner for the adults. The opening of the new BOK Center in downtown Tulsa, less than a mile from the clubhouse, created new opportunities. For the arena's inaugural event, a concert by The Eagles, the club hosted a party with dinner and a shuttle to the BOK Center. The club also turned BOK attractions such as the circus and

July Fourth remains the club's biggest day of the year. In 2008, more than one thousand people celebrated with a picnic, games, golf, the pool, and fireworks.

Longtime member Pat Cremin sizes up the gingerbread house he's building with granddaughter Asia in the 2004 version of a TCC holiday tradition.

the Rockettes into family events with group ticket purchases preceded by activities at the club.

Cards remain popular, too, although perhaps not as pervasive as they once were.

"We have a pretty good core of gin players in the locker room," Fiscus said.

"Many of the older golfers, especially some of the ladies, come out and play cards in cold weather. And, we do have a regular group of ladies that play poker."

But the big event, as it has been for decades, is the Fourth of July.

The Fourth remains the biggest day of the year for the club, with activities that generally include a picnic, music on the outside deck, and fireworks.

The neighborhood around the club was changing, too.

In the late 1990s, a Tulsa firefighter named Terry McGee built eight new upper middle class homes on three vacant acres just east of the course. In 2001, after a decade of discussion and negotiation, the Osage Hills Apartments on the northwest side of the course were demolished to make room for a new development of modest but neat apartments, duplexes, and houses.

The old apartments had been built right after World War II. At the time, they were among the most modern in the city. By the 1980s, though, they had deteriorated into a squalid, crime-ridden slum.

In late 2007, however, the club experienced a much more unpleasant kind of change.

On the night of December 9, the most damaging ice storm in Tulsa's history descended on the city. Great trees exploded with the reverberating booms of an artillery barrage. Lights went out all over the state, and stayed off for days and even weeks. Roofs collapsed under the weight of the falling limbs, windows shattered, utility lines sagged and snapped. Stunned Tulsans came out the next morning to find neighborhoods practically in ruins.

Tulsa Country Club's ancient forest was not spared. Some fifteen hundred trees were damaged, many beyond saving.

"The storm hit us very hard," said Fiscus. "We had more damage than any other course in the area."

Damage to the course and grounds amounted to over $400,000. The golf course had to be closed for two months. Clean-up became a social activity for some of the members.

With the destruction, though, came a renewal. Where trees had to be removed, the extra light and air encouraged thick, lush grass to sprout in the spring. The trees that survived regenerated. Among the few that came through the storm with hardly a scratch was the state's largest lace bark elm, still standing sentry on No. 17.

By early spring, Tulsa Country Club was back to something resembling normal.

The ice storm of December 2007 was the most destructive storm in the city's history and damaged or destroyed 1,500 trees at Tulsa Country Club alone. Crews were brought in from across the United States to restore power and remove debris.

The storm bent, broke, and twisted trees into bizarre shapes.

Members like Sam and Paula Bratton pitched in to help clean up after the December 2007 storm.

Course superintendent Brady Finton stands amid a pile of debris at Tulsa Country Club. Damage to the grounds amounted to over $400,000.

Participants in the centennial hickory shaft tournament gather around the figure of A. W. Tillinghast. Using replica 1920s era equipment, the players also contrived their own period costumes, most notable for an impressive exhibition of argyle socks.

A banquet featuring a multimedia presentation honoring the club's heritage kicked off centennial year activities. Among these was a "turn-back-the-clock" day—a golf tournament using wooden shaft clubs, 1920s era golf balls, and period attire, including plus fours and argyle socks.

The highlight came in late September, when the USGA event so long sought after finally came to town.

Tulsa Country Club's two-and-a-half year quest for a USGA event ended in March 2006 when the club was awarded the 2008 Senior Women's Amateur.

"This is a great event with the senior women," Fiscus told the *World*. "We want to demonstrate to the USGA what kind of first-class event that we're capable of running."

Even with the tournament more than two years away, preparations began almost immediately. A TCC contingent led by general co-chairs Sonya Weese and Lew Erickson went to the 2006 tournament on Sea Island, Georgia, for insights on everything from signage to merchandizing. The following year, in 2007, Fiscus, Combe, and superintendent Brady Finton went to the tournament in Sunriver, Oregon.

Tulsa Country Club, however, was different from those two clubs in at least one very important respect. Sea Island and Sunriver, as resort developments, had corporate staffs to carry out much of the work of putting on a tournament. Sea Island even had its own shirt company. TCC was going to have to rely on volunteers.

"I can't even begin to tell you how many man-hours went into this," Weese said in a 2008 interview. "The volunteer coordinators spent untold hours on the phone and on the computers. We had volunteers from all over the state."

The event brought together 132 of the best amateur women golfers age fifty and over from all over the United States and Canada and as far away as Korea and Spain. Nineteen players advanced to the tournament by benefit of exemptions. The rest of the field qualified at twenty-three sites throughout the country, including Oklahoma City's Quail Creek Golf & Country Club.

The entries included four-time winners Anne Sander—the only woman in the tournament to have played at TCC in the 1960 U.S. Women's Amateur—and Carole Semple Thompson, three-time winner Marlene Streit, two-time winner Diane Lang, former champion Carolyn Creekmore, defending champion

Carolyn Creekmore of Dallas shot a tournament-best 69 during qualifying to win U.S. Senior Women's Amateur medalist honors. She lost to fellow Texan Toni Wiesner in the semifinals.

Anna Schultz, and 2008 Mid-Amateur champion Joan Higgins.

The championship officially began on September 20, although the players began arriving several days in advance for practice rounds and to get acclimated. They could not have found better conditions—mild, calm days and a course at the top of its game, set up to play as a par 71 at 5,760 yards.

Qualifying began on a cool, hazy Saturday morning with the course frosted by dew. Higgins and Noreen Mohler, a Mid-Am semifinalist, each matched par with early tee times and that held up for the first round lead.

The second day belonged to Creekmore. Also teeing off in the morning, she made five birdies, including four on the last nine holes, to turn in a 69 for a 142 total and medalist honors. Higgins and Mohler, playing their second rounds in the afternoon, shot 74 and 79 respectively. Higgins's 145 total left her in second place while Mohler slipped into a third-place tie with Maggie Weder.

A logjam at 162 caused a seven-way playoff for the last four match-play spots. Fortunately, only two holes, played in deepening twilight, were needed to sort out the tie. Among those failing to make the match play bracket was former TCC club champion Patty French.

The first day of match play produced few surprises, although Schultz, the defending champion, was beaten by 2001 runner-up Anne Carr of Seattle. Creekmore defeated one of the previous day's playoff survivors, Mary Flynn, 5-and-4. Higgins beat Spain's Vicky Pertierra by the same score, while Mohler held off Susan Rampelberger 2-and-1. Teresa Delarzelere, the last of three Oklahomans in the tournament, fell to Maggie Scott, 1-up.

Toni Wiesner's steady irons overcame Carolyn Creekmore 2-and-1 in the semifinals to reach the Senior Women's Amateur championship match for the third time.

Two rounds were played on Tuesday, narrowing the field to eight. Those quarterfinalists included Thompson, scheduled for a November induction into the World Golf Hall of Fame, and Creekmore, as well as Higgins, Lang, two-time runner-up Toni Wiesner, Tanna Lee Richard, Claudia Pilot, and Boodie McGurn.

Creekmore still figured to be the favorite, despite two narrow victories. Thompson, who had not played that well until Tuesday, won convincingly, while Higgins and Pilot both continued their strong play. Richard upset Mohler in the third round, while Lang, dismayed by an 80 in her first qualifying round, continued scrapping with a 1-up third-round victory of 2007 runner-up Robyn Puckett.

Toni Wiesner, who had qualified in the middle of the pack with a 157, defeated McGurn 3-and-2 in Wednesday morning's quarterfinal, then shocked the top seed Creekmore 2-and-1 in the afternoon finals to reach her third championship match but first in eight years.

Lang knocked out Higgins 3-and-2 in the quarters and dispatched Pilot 2-up in the semis. Champion in 2005 and 2006, Lang was a former professional from Jamaica who had quit her real estate job to concentrate on winning another Senior Women's Amateur.

Far from overpowering, Wiesner doggedly hung with Creekmore until the latter faltered on the sixteenth and seventeenth holes. Wiesner took the lead on the sixteenth after her second shot, headed for the far left rough, struck a metal yardage marker on the cart path and bounded back into the fairway.

Diane Lang, a native Jamaican living in Florida, defeated Toni Wiesner 6-and-5 to win her third U.S. Senior Women's Amateur title in four years.

Wiesner saved par and took the seventeenth with a conceded par putt to reach the final.

A tall, shambling figure in overalls, a gigantic straw hat, and full beard formed a gallery of one shadowing Wiesner during the latter stages of the tournament. A curious—and incongruous—sight lumbering across the course, he turned out to be a chemical engineer-turned-goat rancher named Joe Mundis, who had caddied for Wiesner in the 1987 Women's Mid-Amateur at Southern Hills.

Guile and precision carried Wiesner into the finals at Tulsa Country Club but could carry her no further. Lang, tall and tan and eight years younger than Wiesner, won the first two holes and stood six-up after ten holes. A sixteen-foot par putt on thirteen gave her the match, 6-and-5.

"This makes all the hard work worthwhile," Lang told the USGA's Craig Smith. "I put in a lot of sweat and tears over the last year to get my name on that trophy again. For a little girl from Jamaica, that ain't half bad."

"I don't seem to be able to put it together in the final," Wiesner said, also to Smith. "Maybe I put too much pressure on myself. I just couldn't get off the tee today."

The championship was as successful for Tulsa Country Club as it was for Lang. Praise for the course, the club's organization, the accommodations, and, of course, the people, was unanimous.

"I think everything went exceptionally well," Weese said a few days after the tournament. "I've already received three or four letters from members of the USGA. One said they had been on the committee for nine years and this was about the best tournament yet."

Teresa Belmont, USGA assistant director for women's competitions, said her only reservation was leaving behind so many new friends.

U.S. Senior Women's Amateur champion Diane Lang and her trophy hitch a ride with assistant superintendent Gary Heimbach.

U.S. Senior Women's Amateur general co-chairs Lew Erickson, left, and Sonya Weese with champion Diane Lang at the awards presentation.

Greta Heslet beat TCC to a centennial, celebrating her one-hundredth birthday at the club on December 16, 2005.

"The players loved it," Belmont said. "They had nothing but praise for the course, for the hospitality, and for the friendliness of the volunteers. And it was the same with the committee and the USGA.

"Everything was great. We didn't have any major tweaking to do with the course. And whoever was in charge of the weather did a great job."

From the club's standpoint, it was a chance to see outstanding golfers—and to show off a little.

"I like showing other players what this club is about," said Combe. "I think our members like hearing the rave reviews. It's very satisfying.

"This club has put itself in a situation that if it wanted to propose hosting another championship, I think it would get it."

In its centennial year, Tulsa Country Club once again asked itself the Eternal Question: What would Tillie do?

In March 2008, the club announced it was hiring golf architect Rees Jones to develop a plan for improvements to the course in keeping with Tillinghast's original concept. By fall, those plans were being finalized for presentation to the membership.

The biggest changes would involve creating five tees for every hole, making the course more enjoyable to a wider range of players, and eliminating many of the raised edges around the greens, which are contrary to a Tillinghast design. Several tee boxes would be shifted to relieve congestion and improve safety.

But most of the current holes, said Combe, are very much like Tillinghast built ninety years ago.

"Twelve to thirteen holes haven't changed much at all," he said. "They've held onto the same integrity as far as where they are and how they're played."

But, Combe added, "Over the years, the Tillinghast concept has been lost on some of the course. If the members decide to do this, it would restore a lot of the Tillinghast values. The club would be more than one hundred years old. Not many clubs can say they're one hundred years old."

"Who decided a golf course should have eighteen holes?" asked Phil Doherty. "Why not fifteen?"

It seems that on this particular day—a cool, overcast, windy day—the former club president wished he could have deleted at least three holes from his round. Whether this sentiment reflected on the quality of his play or a desire to reach the comfort of the Trophy Room a little sooner was not clear. Certainly, he had reason for the latter. For, while a blustery north wind blew the little white ball to and fro, in the clubhouse his fellow past presidents were gathering to complete what has become an annual ritual.

Every October, the current and past presidents of Tulsa Country Club meet for lunch, a round of golf, and some laughs. In 2008, about a dozen of them were there, trading stories and bragging—or complaining—about their golf games.

A. B. Steen, the 1982 club president, said the thing about Tulsa Country Club is that you can go out and play a round of golf, have fun, and not worry what somebody thinks about your swing.

"When I was promoted to president of my company, they wanted me to join Southern Hills. I said, 'Well, that's okay, but I'd as soon keep playing my golf at Tulsa Country Club.'"

That, maybe as much as anything, explains the club's longevity. It also says something about its prospects for the future.

"When people come here, they notice the closeness," said 2007 president Tom Chitwood. "Everybody knows just about everybody else."

"A country club is more than bricks and mortar," he said. "It's people."

TCC members Yvette and Justin Bray enjoy the 2008 Centennial Gala.

TCC fixtures Don Eustice, right, and Jim Unruh look over club memorabilia during the Centennial Gala. Unruh's wife Paula Unruh is facing the camera.

Grant Holley and Dylan Wilson poised for action prior to TCC's 2008 Easter egg hunt.

The first Tulsa Country Club pool was built in 1935. They've been popular with kids and their parents ever since.

TCC's 2008 junior golfers.

Bench in memory of Edith Rowe, given by the TCC Women's Golf Association.

Hole #1

Hole #2

Hole #3

Hole #4

Hole #5

Hole #6

Hole #7

Hole #8

Hole #9

Hole #10

Hole #11

Hole #12

Hole #13

Hole #14

Hole #15

Hole #16

Hole #17

Hole #18

TCC's annual hayride drew a wagonload and then some during the last weekend of October 2008.

TCC member Mary Johnson and 2008's littlest hayrider, son Will Johnson.

Sack race at the July Fourth Picnic

David Thompson and guest Scott McNeal at the 2007 Tillinghast Invitational.

TCC cook Brian Polm, Executive Chef Michael Hobbs and Sous Chef Frank Brown.

Golf professional Jeff Combe visits with Tom Russell during the annual July 4th Putting Contest.

TCC member Harvey Blumenthal.

The annual Halloween Hayride and Costume Party is always a hit with the Club's kids.

Left to right: Golf Professional Jeff Combe, Golf Course Superintendent Brady Finton, Service Director Alex Stodghill, and General Manager Jason Fiscus celebrate the Club's Centennial.

A wedding ceremony overlooking the TCC golf course and downtown skyline.

Past president Bailey Word celebrates July 4th, the Club's largest annual gathering.

The "Tillinghouse"

Long-time TCC members Tom and Biddy Kupke.

Only Santa knows if this youngster asked for more than his two front teeth.

APPENDIX A: CLUB PRESIDENTS

1908 F. A. Leovy
1909 E. Rogers Kemp
1910 E. Rogers Kemp
1911 H. Y. "Cap" Arnold
1912 H. Y. "Cap" Arnold
1913 H. Y. "Cap" Arnold
1914 H. Y. "Cap" Arnold
1915 H. Y. "Cap" Arnold
1916 H. Y. "Cap" Arnold
1917 H. Y. "Cap" Arnold
1918 H. Y. "Cap" Arnold
1919 Bert Collins
1920 Bert Collins
1921 Bert Collins
1922 Dana Kelsey
1923 Dana Kelsey
1924 Dana Kelsey
1925 Dana Kelsey
1926 Dana Kelsey
1927 Dana Kelsey
1928 S. G. Kennedy
1929 S. G. Kennedy
1930 Frank Rodolf
1931 Frank Rodolf
1932 Frank Rodolf
1933 Frank Rodolf
1934 Frank Rodolf
1935 Dana Kelsey
1936 Dana Kelsey
1937 E. H. Leroux
1938 E. H. Leroux
1939 E. H. Leroux
1940 E. H. Leroux
1941 E. H. Leroux
1942 E. H. Leroux
1943 E. H. Leroux
1944 E. H. Leroux
1945 E. H. Leroux
1946 E. H. Leroux
1947 E. H. Leroux
1948 LeRoy Sipes
1949 LeRoy Sipes
1950 F. Lee Murdock
1951 Fred Robbins
1952 M. D. Gilbert (resigned)
1952 T. H. Riggin
1953 T. H. Riggin
1954 T. H. Riggin
1955 J. C. Hamilton
1956 F. Lee Murdock
1957 F. Lee Murdock
1958 F. Lee Murdock
1959 L. C. "Bud" Woods
1960 T. H. Riggin
1961 T. H. Riggin
1962 T. H. Riggin
1963 T. H. Riggin
1964 T. H. Riggin
1965 T. H. Riggin
1966 T. H. Riggin
1967 Fred Robbins
1968 C. Page "Pinky" Stanley
1969 Paul J. Vaananen
1970 Forrest Shoemaker Jr.
1971 James Unruh
1972 F. P. Mueller
1973 D. L. Potter
1974 G. B. Gilliam
1975 Donald F. Brown Jr.
1976 Gerald M. Bauer
1977 William G. Swartz
1978 Thomas L. Smith Jr.
1979 James R. Newlin
1980 Robert C. Little
1981 George S. Battles
1982 A. B. Steen
1983 L. Dean Cox
1984 Richard E. Wright III
1985 Raymond L. Tullius
1986 L. Bailey Word
1987 Richard T. Garren
1988 Rex J. Williams
1989 Thomas Rinehart
1990 Forrest Shoemaker Jr.
1991 Philip Doherty
1992 Ed Fariss
1993 Frank Enzbrenner
1994 Blake Atkins
1995 Jack L. Bentley
1996 James M. King
1997 Michael Perry
1998 Philip Doherty
1999 Paul Zaloudik
2000 Timothy F. Breedlove
2001 Steve Austin
2002 Rick Walters
2003 Paul Sizemore
2004 Steve Stecher
2005 Paul Williams
2006 Rob Irwin
2007 Tom Chitwood
2008 David Thompson

APPENDIX B: TCC COURSE 1920-67

(Don Eustice first played the Tulsa Country Club course as a boy during the 1930s. During an October 2007 interview, he offered some recollections of the course before it was reordered in 1968).

Old No. 16, new No. 1

The No. 16 tee was well back from where No. 1 is now. There was a dogleg to the right, and the green was about one hundred yards north of the new one.

Old No. 17, new No. 2

The old No. 17 tee box is still visible just left of the current No. 1 fairway where it turns to southwest. The old pro's house and shed were on the old seventeen. The stream there was sometimes fifteen feet deep and twenty feet wide.

The old seventeen wasn't as bad as it appears. You had to hit a pretty good hook. A lot of people had problems hitting it on the road (Edison Street). When Nelson played here, he teed off, caught a tree, and the ball kicked right out there in the fairway. He took out his No. 2 and hit it to the green (250 yards). Back then we didn't have golf clubs that could go that far.

Old No. 18, new No. 3

The green's been moved back. Old-timers used to say it was the only hole ever played where you could three-putt with a wedge in between.

What made this hole hard was that you had to hit through a narrow opening. If you didn't go through there, you were in trouble. The green was about one hundred yards shorter then.

Old No. 1, new No. 4

They can change it, they can do all sorts of things to it, but they can't run me off.

Old No. 7, new No. 5

There used to be a ditch and some pines on the right. If you pushed your tee shot to the right, you did not have a shot.

Old No. 8, new No. 6

A beautiful little hole.

Old No. 9, new No. 7

A dogleg.

Old No. 10, new No. 8

The green was a sharp dogleg right.

Old No. 6, new No. 15

A little gem. It's kind of a deceiving hole. One of Tillinghast's trademarks was that most of his greens were elevated like this one. That's just one of the little things that can get your attention.

Old No. 2, new No. 16

They used to land airplanes off to the right of the fairway. We had kite-flying contests there in the summer.

APPENDIX C: NOTABLE TOURNAMENTS AT TCC

Date	Tournament	Winner
1910	Oklahoma Open	William Nichols
1910	Oklahoma Men's Amateur	Harry Gwinnup
1912	Oklahoma Open	Chester Nelson
1912	Oklahoma Men's Amateur	Harry Gwinnup
1920	Oklahoma Men's Amateur	James Kennedy
1920	Oklahoma Open	Bill Mehlhorn
1923	Oklahoma Open	Bill Mehlhorn
1925	Oklahoma Open	Ed Dudley
1927	Oklahoma Open	Dick Grout
1930	Trans-Mississippi Women's Championship	Mrs. Hulbert Clarke
1931	Oklahoma Open	Emmett J. Rogers
1934	Oklahoma Women's Amateur	Estelle Drennan
1938	Oklahoma Women's Amateur	Joyce Wallace
1948	Oklahoma Women's Amateur	Patti Blanton
1948	Oklahoma Open	Jimmy Gauntt
1953	Oklahoma Men's Amateur	Leonard Young
1956	Oklahoma Men's Amateur	Harold Corbett
1959	Oklahoma Women's Amateur	Dale Fleming
1960	U.S. Women's Amateur	JoAnne Gunderson
1965	Oklahoma Men's Amateur	Bob Dickson
1968	Oklahoma Women's Amateur	Dale Fleming McNamara
1973	Oklahoma Men's Amateur	Dave Barr
1981	Oklahoma Women's Amateur	Patty Coatney
1984	Roy Clark Senior PGA	Miller Barber
1986	Oklahoma Men's Amateur	Mike Hughett (stroke)
		Kyle Flinton (match)
1993	Oklahoma Men's Amateur (stroke play)	Tim Graves
1996	Oklahoma Women's Amateur	Sheila Dills
1999	NCAA Division I Women	Duke (team)
		Grace Park (ind)
2001	Williams LPGA Championship	Gloria Park
2002	Williams LPGA Championship	Annika Sorenstam
2003	John Q. Hammons LPGA	Karrie Webb
2008	U.S. Senior Women's Amateur	Diane Lang

APPENDIX D: CLUB CHAMPIONS

Men
1908 Frank Moore
1912 Charles Bliss
1913 Charles Bliss
1914 James Kennedy
1915 Harry Gwinnup
1916 Harry Gwinnup
1917 Cliff Bass
1918 E. P. Bates
1919 G. A. Matson
1920 Cliff Bass
1921 James Kennedy
1922 Don Bothwell
1923 Charles Bassl
1925 George Johnston
1926 James Kennedy
1927 John Winters
1928 George Johnston
1929 Lee Kennedy
1930 Lee Kennedy
1931 Fred Daniel
1932 Fred Daniel
1933 Lee Kennedy
1934 John Risk
1935 Earl Berryhill
1936 J. K. Thompson
1937 R. E. Thompson
1938 J. K. Thompson
1939 Lon Beddoe
1940 Dick Mason
1941 James Duck
1942 John N. Martin
1943 Dwight Skaggs
1944 Reed Alsop Jr.
1945 Reed Alsop Jr.
1946 Leo Case
1947 B. C. Coffman
1948 H. E. Staples Jr.
1949 Oscar Grimes
1950 Oscar Grimes
1951 Oscar Grimes
1952 Paul Reitz
1953 H. E. Staples Jr.
1954 Jack Judd
1955 J. C. Hamilton
1956 Walter Emery
1957 D. R. Winslow
1958 Jim Moeller
1959 Fred Mock Jr.
1960 Fred Mock Jr.
1961 Stanford Hall
1962 Walter Emery
1963 Mac Conine
1964 John W. Marshall
1965 D. R. Winslow
1966 John Miller
1967 Jim Unruh
1968 C. S. Hightower
1969 Gerry Phillips
1970 Jim Unruh
1971 Jim Unruh
1972 Jim Unruh
1973 Forrest Shoemaker Jr.
1974 Jim Young
1975 Jerry Harris
1976 Forrest Shoemaker Jr.
1977 Jim Unruh
1978 Jim Young
1979 Don Ward
1980 Jim Unruh
1981 Eric Mueller
1982 Fred Lawson
1983 Eric Mueller
1984 Jim Young
1985 Jim Unruh
1986 Mike Hughett
1987 Eric Mueller
1988 Eric Mueller
1989 Mike Hughett
1990 Eric Mueller
1991 Eric Mueller
1992 Mike Hughett
1993 Eric Mueller
1994 Eric Mueller
1995 Blake Atkins
1996 Mike Hughett
1997 Brett Pratt
1998 Murphy Mitchell
1999 Murphy Mitchell
2000 Brad Watts
2001 Murphy Mitchell
2002 Tom Zeiders
2003 Tom Zeiders
2004 Tom Zeiders
2005 Murphy Mitchell
2006 Bailey Word
2007 Carter Johnson
2008 Murphy Mitchell

Women
1935 Mrs. L. L. Van Zandt
1936 Mrs. L. L. Van Zandt
1937 No record
1938 Mrs. J. L. Ferguson
1939 Mrs. L. L. Van Zandt
1940 Mrs. C. M. Severns
1941 Mrs. C. M. Severns
1942 Margaret Thompson
1943 Mrs. C. P. Dudley
1944 Mrs. C. P. Dudley
1945 Mrs. L. G. Sutter
1946 Mrs. L. G. Sutter
1947 Mrs. L. G. Sutter
1948 Mrs. L. G. Sutter
1949 Mrs. L. G. Sutter
1950 Margaret Larkins
1951 Mrs. R. C. Hall
1952 No record
1953 Mrs. R. C. Hall
1954 Mrs. R. C. Hall
1955 Mrs. R. C. Hall
1956 Mrs. Ed E. Oberholtzer
1957 Mrs. R. C. Hall
1958 Gerry Adamson
1959 Gwen Brownlee
1960 Mrs. R. C. Hall
1961 Mrs. R. C. Hall
1962 Mrs. R. C. Hall
1963 Mrs. R. C. Hall
1964 Mrs. R. C. Hall
1965 Mrs. R. C. Hall
1966 Mrs. R. C. Hall
1967 Mrs. J. R. Biddick
1968 Mrs. J. R. Biddick
1969 Mrs. J. R. Biddick
1970 Mrs. J. R. Biddick
1971 Mrs. D. F. Brown
1972 Laura Goodman
1973 Dottie Biddick
1974 Mrs. D. F. Brown
1975 Mrs. D. F. Brown
1976 Mrs. E. E. Bonsper
1977 Mrs. G. S. Whitaker Jr.
1978 Mrs. E. E. Bonsper
1979 Mrs. E. E. Bonsper
1980 Mrs. G. S. Whitaker Jr.
1981 Mrs. E. E. Bonsper
1982 Mrs. E. E. Bonsper
1983 Mrs. E. E. Bonsper
1984 Mrs. E. E. Bonsper
1985 Mrs. E. E. Bonsper
1986 Trudy McKenzie
1987 Mrs. E. E. Bonsper
1988 Lew Erickson
1989 Mrs. William French
1990 Mrs. William French
1991 Mrs. William French
1992 Mrs. William French
1993 Mrs. William French
1994 Mrs. William French
1995 Mrs. William French
1996 Joanne Heller
1997 Mary Harvey
1998 Joanne Heller
1999 Mary Harvey
2000 Cindy Short
2001 Dianna Patterson
2002 Mary Harvey
2003 Mary Harvey
2004 Mary Harvey
2005 Helen Kern
2006 Lisa Emery
2007 Lisa Emery
2008 Sonya Weese

BIBLIOGRAPHY

"Ailing Country Club." *Wall Street Journal*, Dec. 28, 1961.

Barkow, Al. *Gettin' to the Dance Floor: An Oral History of American Golf*. New York: Atheneum, 1986.

Blakely, Jule. "Tulsa Country Club Opening Is Successful." *Tulsa World*, Mar. 19, 1968.

Brick, Howard. *Age of Contradiction: American Thought and Culture in the 1960s*. New York: Twayne Publishers, 1998.

Bridgewater, B. A. "Consistent Game Wins Golf Title for Mrs. Clarke." *Tulsa World*, June 8, 1930.

———. "Golf Favorites Compete Today in Semifinals." *Tulsa World*, June 6, 1930.

———. "Jim Kennedy Leads Field of 110 and Is Medalist in Club Championship." *Tulsa World*, Oct. 10, 1921.

———. "John Winters Leading State Open Field." *Tulsa World*, Sept. 13, 1931.

———. "Telling the World." *Tulsa World*, Sept. 14, 1944.

———. "Telling the World." *Tulsa World*, May 3, 1945.

Brown, Phillip W. "Remembrances of My Grandfather." The Tillinghast Association.

Charvat, Jack. "Sports Slants." *Tulsa Tribune*, July 20, 1956.

"Chicago Architect Begins Work on New Golf Course for Country Club." *Tulsa World*, May 1, 1917.

"The Country Club." *Tulsa World*, Apr. 25, 1908.

"Country Club Golf at Standstill as Committee Absent." *Tulsa Tribune*, Apr. 7, 1920.

"Country Club Is Destroyed." *Tulsa World*, Feb. 2, 1916.

"Country Club to Open New House." *Tulsa World*, Feb. 18, 1917.

"Country Club to Rebuild at Once." *Tulsa World*, Feb. 3, 1916.

Crawley, Bill. "M'Namara Wins Fourth State Crown." *Tulsa World*, June 8, 1968.

———. "Mrs. Morse's 75 Wins State Medal." *Tulsa World*, June 4, 1968.

Cronley, Jay. "McNamara Belts Par by 4, Romps to Win in State Golf." *Tulsa Tribune*, June 8, 1968.

Dailey, Larry. "Kennedy Defeats Gwinnup for Amateur Golf Honors." *Tulsa World*, Oct. 22, 1920.

Davidson, Sara A., ed. "Society." *Tulsa Democrat*, Feb. 1, 1916.

Doyle, Matt. "TCC to Host Women's Golf Event in 2008." *Tulsa World*, Mar. 24, 2006.

———. "Webb Standing Firm." *Tulsa World*, Sept. 7, 2003.

———. "Wire-to-Wire." *Tulsa World*, Sept. 8, 2003.

"Dr. Kennedy's Rites Will Be Held Today; Came to Tulsa in '91." *Tulsa World*, Sept. 29, 1941.

Farber, David, and Beth Bailey. *The Columbia Guide to America in the 1960s*. New York: Columbia University Press, 2001.

"1st Meet Set for New TCC." *Tulsa World*, June 2, 1968.

Foresman, Bob. "Cattle Were Just a Natural Hazard at Tulsa's First Country Club." *Tulsa Tribune*, Aug. 23, 1964.

Gideon, Russell. "New Southside Country Club Planned by Tulsa Leaders." *Tulsa World*, Dec. 31, 1934.

Gilstrap, Harry. "Best-Balanced List in History Competes Here." *Tulsa World*, June 2, 1930.

———. "State Champs Remain in Quest for Golf Crown." *Tulsa World*, June 5, 1930.

Goble, Danney. *Tulsa! Biography of the American City*. Tulsa: Council Oak Books, 1997.

"Golf Tournament of Country Club Saturday." *Tulsa Democrat*, Sept. 3, 1908.

"Golf Tournament Score." *Tulsa Democrat*, Sept. 30, 1905.

Goodwin, Stephen, and Ricke Wolffe. "The Creator of Golf Courses." The Tillinghast Association.

Haisten, Bill. "Course 'Demands Patience,'" *Tulsa World*, Sept. 2, 2001.

———. "Donna's Delight." *Tulsa World*, Sept. 9, 2001.

———. "Feels Like a Major." *Tulsa World*, Sept. 8, 2001.

———. "No Surprise—It's Annika." *Tulsa World*, Sept. 9, 2002.

———. "Par Is Lost in Prime Conditions." *Tulsa World*, May 20, 1999.

———. "Sorenstam Surges to the Top." *Tulsa World*, Sept. 8, 2002.

———. "Uncertainty Dots Williams Tourney." *Tulsa World*, Sept. 1, 2002.

Hannigan, Frank. "Golf's Forgotten Genius." *Golf Journal*, May 1974.

———. "Tillie Leaves a Legacy." *Golf Digest*, Aug. 1997.

Hartzell, Bob. "Golf Always Was Fun Game for Emery." *Tulsa Tribune*, June 28, 1973.

Henry, Clay. "Barber Remedies Logjam." *Tulsa World*, June 18, 1984.

———. "January Will Cut Senior Stops Himself if Organizers Refuse to." *Tulsa World*, June 15, 1984.

———. "Moody Motivated by Tour Money." *Tulsa World*, June 8, 1984.

———. "Morrish's Touch Gives TCC New Look from Old Master." *Tulsa World*, Sept. 18, 1988.

———. "Silvestrone Defies Logic by Leading." *Tulsa World*, June 16, 1984.

———. "TCC Changes Enhance Original Design." *Tulsa World*, Aug. 18, 1985.

Hoover, John E. "Andrews Saw the Unexpected." *Tulsa World*, Sept. 10, 2001.

"Initial Tournament of Oklahoma Golf Association." *Tulsa Democrat*, May 23, 1910.

"It's a Woman's World of Fashion." *Tulsa World*, Feb. 29, 1968.

Kensler, Tom. "Flinton Passes Amateur Test." *The Oklahoman*, June 22, 1986.

———. "Name Players Fall as Flinton, Mase Reach Final." *The Oklahoman*, June 21, 1986.

Klein, John. "LPGA Golfers Embrace Tulsa Visit." *Tulsa World*, Aug. 25, 1998.

———. "LPGA, Tulsa Reunited." *Tulsa World*, Sept. 11, 2001.

———. "Tulsa Golf History Is Repeated Again." *Tulsa World*, Sept. 10, 2001.

Krehbiel, Randy. *Tulsa's Daily World: The Story of a Newspaper and Its Town*. Tulsa: World Publishing Co., 2007.

"Ky Laffoon." Ozark Fairways.

Lemon, Del. *The Story of Golf in Oklahoma*. Norman, Okla.: University of Oklahoma Press, 2001.

Lester, Terrell. "Golf Champ Didn't Conquer All Holes." *Tulsa World*, July 24, 1965.

Linihan, Richard. "Mr. X Has Close Call." *Tulsa Tribune*, June 18, 1984.

Lobaugh, Tom. "Angry Barr Wins State Amateur Golf." *Tulsa World*, June 30, 1973.

———. "Barr Gets 3-Shot Lead in State Amateur Golf." *Tulsa World*, June 29, 1973.

———. "Barr Tops Amateur by Two Strokes." *Tulsa World*, June 28, 1973.

———. "Cigar Derby Signals a Return to the Dog Days for TCC Group." *Tulsa World*, July 11, 1976.

———. "Cullen Loves New Job at Sweetwater Course." *Tulsa World*, June 19, 1983.

———. "DeLozier Set to Defend." *Tulsa World*, June 24, 1973.

———. "Facelifting Due at TCC in Fall." *Tulsa World*, July 9, 1967.

———. "Jo Ann Grimes Is Girls' Medalist at TCC with 92." *Tulsa World*, June 1, 1950.

"Low Scores at the Golf Meet." *Tulsa Democrat*, May 26, 1910.

Macklin, Beth. "'Impossible Dream' Donations Coming in." *Tulsa World*, Aug. 29, 1984.

MacLeod, Ken. "Buyers' Market on the Course." *Tulsa Tribune*, Mar. 27, 1992.

———. "TU's Laitinen Prevails in Photo Finish." *Tulsa World*, Oct. 8, 1998.

"Magazine Features Four Tulsa Homes." *Tulsa Tribune*, Mar. 2, 1959.

Mayo, James M. *The American Country Club: Its Origins and Development*. New Brunswick, N.J.: Rutgers University, 1998.

"Mehlhorn Plans Spring Tourneys." *Tulsa World*, Mar. 14, 1920.

"Muskogee Wins Golf Honors." *Tulsa World*, May 28, 1910.

"New Club House to Be Better Than Old." *Tulsa Democrat*, Feb. 2, 1916.

"New Home of Tulsa Country Club?" *Tulsa Tribune*, Feb. 19, 1966.

"Notepad." *Tulsa World*, Sept. 8, 2001.

O'Kane, Dan. "Duke and Relativity." *Tulsa World*, May 20, 1999.

———. "LPGA a Good Fit for Tulsa." *Tulsa World*, Aug. 24, 1998.

———. "Nick Shooting for Sixth Consecutive OGA Title." *Tulsa World*, July 27, 1993.

———. "Pro Tour Wants to Play at TCC, Maybe in 2000." *Tulsa World*, May 24, 1999.

———. "Tax Law Changes Unpopular with Country Clubs." *Tulsa World*, Aug. 22, 1993.

———. "TCC Courting a USGA Event." *Tulsa World*, May 6, 2004.

———. "Tulsa Gets Women's NCAA Golf Tourney." *Tulsa World*, Aug. 15, 1997.

Owens, Jesse. "Tulsan Sees Golf Boom from Home near TCC." *Tulsa World*, Aug. 8, 1976.

Peper, George, ed. *Golf in America: The First One Hundred Years*. New York: Harry N. Abrams, 1987.

Perkins, Lilian C. "Society: Clubs, Music & Women's Work." *Tulsa World*, Oct. 24, 1920.

"Picture Story of Tulsa Home Runs 6 Pages." *Tulsa Tribune*, Apr. 7, 1957.

"Recreation in Indian Territory." *Sturm's State Magazine* vol. 1, no. 2 (October 1905).

Rodolf, Frank. Statement to Tulsa Country Club stockholders, Jan. 15, 1934.

"A Scotch Teacher." *Tulsa World*, Sept. 30, 1908.

"Seniors Golf Tickets Sales Under Way." *Tulsa World*, June 3, 1984.

Smith, Craig. "Lang Beats Wiesner for USGA Senior Women's Amateur Title, 6 and 5." U.S. Golf Association, Sept. 25, 2008.

"Society News." *Tulsa World*, May 2, 1917.

"Southern Hills Chooses 16 Associate Directors; Plans to Be Ready Feb. 10." *Tulsa World*, Jan. 6, 1935.

Strege, John. *When War Played Through: Golf During World War II*. New York: Gotham, 2005.

"TCC to Buy Site and Add Acres." *Tulsa World*, Nov. 29, 1956.

"The Team Is Chosen." *Tulsa World*, Sept. 9, 1908.

"Thompson Wins Title Over Veteran, 3 and 2." *Tulsa World*, July 22, 1962.

Tillinghast, A. W. *Gleanings from the Wayside: My Recollections as a Golf Architect*. Short Hills, N.J.: TreeWolf Productions, 2001.

———. *Reminiscences of the Links: A Treasury of Essays and Photographs on Scottish and Early American Golf*. Short Hills, N.J.: TreeWolf Productions, 1998.

"Tournament at Country Club." *Tulsa World*, May 24, 1910.

"The Tulsa Club Is Organized." *Tulsa Democrat*, Mar. 17, 1908.

"Tulsa Club Must Restrict Members." *Tulsa World*, Nov. 15, 1936.

Tulsa Country Club Board of Directors minutes, Jan. 18, 1944.

———. Feb. 25, 1958.

———. Jan. 20, 1959.

———. Apr. 28, 1959.

"Tulsa Country Club Is Active." *Tulsa Democrat*, Jan. 24, 1906.

"Tulsa Oil Men Talk Country Club." *Tulsa World*, Oct. 26, 1907.

"Tulsans Told: Get Politically Involved." *Tulsa World*, June 26, 1973.

Turner, John. "Nelson 68, Snead 69 at TCC." *Tulsa World*, May 9, 1945.

———. "Record Field to Start in Women's Golf Today." *Tulsa World*, June 7, 1948.

———. "Schneiter's 68 Topples M'Spaden and Nelson." *Tulsa World*, Sept. 14, 1944.

Typescript. Tulsa Country Club files, undated.

"Welcome Sign Will Be Hung on New Country Club within Few Days Now: Plan New Golf Course of 18 Holes." *Tulsa Democrat*, Feb. 18, 1917.

"Will Organize a Country Club." *Tulsa Democrat*, June 6, 1905.

Williams, Rex J. "President's Address to Tulsa Country Club Membership." 1988 Annual Report.

"Wins the Loving Cup." *Tulsa Democrat*, Oct. 23, 1905.

Wood, G. M. "Country Club and Tulsa Club Working on Plan." *Tulsa Tribune*, Oct. 30, 1934.

———. "Down the Middle Aisle of Sports." *Tulsa Tribune*, Nov. 21, 1936.

Word, Bailey. President's Address to Tulsa Country Club membership, club newsletter, January 1987.

PHOTO CREDITS

(listed by page number)

Beryl Ford/Rotary Club of Tulsa Collection: 10, 11, 24 (top), 25, 26, 28.
Getty Images courtesy LPGA: 46.
PGA: 23, 27 (both), 38, 39, 40 (top), 42, 50 (top), 71 (both), 72 (top), 73 (top).
South Central Golf Magazine: 36.
Tulsa Country Club: cover, front, back, 8, 12 (both), 13, 14, 19, 29, 31, 32 (top), 34, 35, 40 (bottom), 41, 45, 49, 50 (bottom), 53, 54, 55 (both), 58, 59, 61, 64, 65 (all), 66, 67, 72 (bottom), 73 (top center, top right, center right, bottom), 74, 82, 84, 96, 97, 98 (both), 99 (both), 100 (top), 103 (bottom), 104–115 (all).

Tulsa Fire Department: 16–17.
Tulsa Tribune/Tulsa Democrat: 15, 22.
Tulsa World: 24 (center), 32 (center), 40 (center), 43, 48, 52, 56, 62, 70, 77, 78, 79, 88, 89.
U.S. Golf Association: 59, 100 (bottom), 101, 102, 103 (top).

INDEX

Page numbers in italics refer to photos.

A

A. G. Spalding & Co., 13
Abercrombie & Fitch, 38
American Airlines, 44–45
Anderson, H. P., 9, 11, 12
Andrews, Donna, 90, 93–95
Anschutz, Jody Rosenthal, 84–85
Arizona State University, 49, 85–86
Armstrong, W. M., 15
Arnold, H. Y. "Cap," 11, 16, 27
Ashby, H. C., 12
Ashley, Jean, 50
Atkins, Blake, 7
Augusta National Golf Club, 27, 38, 44
Avery, Cyrus, 11, 25

B

Bailey, Keith, 87–88
Baker, Todd, 78
Baltusrol Golf Club, 19
Bank of Oklahoma, 15
Barber, Miller, 72
Barnes, Jim, 26
Barnett, Orville, *54*
Barr, Dave, 68
Basolo, Susan, 63
Bass, C. W., 24
Battles, George, 69–70
Bauer, Beth, 85
Beeler, Lucy, 63
Bell, Clarissa, 10
Belmont, Teresa, 102, 104
Benjamin, Chuck, *54*
Benn, Megan, 84
Berg, Patty, 49
Berning, Sue Maxwell, 48, 57, 59
Biddick, Dottie, 49
Blakely, Julie, 62
Blanton, Patti, *36*, 45, 49, 63
Blumenthal, Harvey, *114*
Boardman, Margaret, 45
BOK Center, 96
"Bouncing Billy," 13
Bowman, Oscar, 31
Box, Montie, 7
Bradstreet, Delight, 26
Brady, Tate, 11
Bratton, Sam and Paula, *99*
Bray, Yvette and Justin, *105*
Bredouw, Mrs. Jack, 55
Bridges, John, 52
Bridgewater, B. A., 21, 30, 31, 32, 39–41
Brown, Frank, *114*
Brownlee, Leslie, 14
Bryan, Dave, 75

C

Campbell, Wallace, 11
Carr, Anne, 101
Casper, Billy, 71
Cedar Ridge Country Club, 62, 64, 70, 79
Children's Medical Center, 70, 72
Chitwood, Tom, 7, 105
Chuasiripron, Jenny, 85
Civil Works Administration, 33
Clark, Roy, 70–72
Clarke, Mrs. Hulbert, 30
Cochran, Bob, 58
Coiner, Dick, *54*
Collins, Bob, 40
Collins, J. C. "Jock," 22, 24
Collins, Joe, 22
Combe, Jeff, 7, *87*, 88, 90, 95, 100, 104–105, *114*
Condon, Glenn, 15
Connors, Bill, 71
Cook, Buddy, 70
Cook, W. A., 10
Corbett, Harold, 51–52
Cornish, Geoffrey S., 20
Crawley, Bill, 63
Creager, Mack, 52
Creed, Clifford Ann, 59
Creekmore, Carolyn, 100–101
Cremin, Pat, 7, 53, 70, 80, 96, *97*
Cremin-Smith, Billie, 70
Crenshaw, Ben, 68
Cronley, Jay, 63
Crosbie, J. E., 11
Crosby, Bing, 39, 44
Cullen, Betsy, 7, *46*, 47–49, 57
Cullen, Ronald, 48
Curtis Cup, 49, 59

D

Dahlman, Joe, 34–35
Dahlman, Richard, 34
Dailey, Larry, 24
Dalasin, Dorothy, 10
Dalton, Emmett, 9
David, Patty, 47, 50
Davidson, R. L., 11
Dayton Last Company (MacGregor Golf), 13
Delarzelere, Teresa, 101
Delasin, Dorothy, 95
DeLozier, Henry, 68
Dickson, Ben, Jr., 60
Dickson, Ben, Sr., 60
Dickson, Bob, 60
Diegel, Leo, *23*
Dillman, Sue Gail, 48
Dills, Joey, 68
Dills, Sheila Luginbuel, 84, *91*
Dodson, Steve, 68
Doherty, Phil, 7, 105
Doyle, Matt, 95
Drennan, Estelle, 29, 49
Duck, Jimmy, 40
Dudley, Ed, 27, 44
Duke University, 85–86
Dunn, Billy "Cotton," 52

E

Edwards, Hank, 68
Elder, Mrs. John, 55
Eller, Judy, 49–50
Emery, Walter, 31–33, 51–52
Erensen, Tim, 95
Erickson, Lew, 100, *103*
Ervine, Ann, 47
Ervine, Bob, 47
Espinosa, Al, *23*
Eustice, Don, 7, 34, 83, *105*
Evans, Charles "Chick," 19, 21, 24
Evans, Fran, 93

F

Farley, Floyd, 30, 62
Farmer, A. L., 11
Farrar, Kathy, 59
Farrell, Johnny, *23*
Fennell, Earl, 52
Fife, Natasha, 59
Finger, Joe, 62
Finton, Brady, *99*, 100, *114*
Fiscus, Jason, 7, 96–98, 100, *114*
Fladoos, Sharon, 49
Flinton, Kyle, 78
Flynn, Mary, 101
Francisco, Sandy, 48
French, Patty, 101

G

Gaillardia Golf and Country Club, 88
Galbreath, Bob, 10
Gallagher, John P. "Jack," 53
Gallagher, Pat, 7, 53
Gann, Buck, 41–42
Gannaway, Charles, Jr., 55
Gauntt, Jimmy, 45
Georgia, University of, 86
Ghezzi, Vic, 44
Gilbert, M. D., 54
Gilliam, Burt, 67
Glenn, J. S., 12
Golden, Johnny, *23*
Golf Club of Oklahoma, 78, 79
Goodwin, Stephen, 20
Goolsby, Phil, 42
Gore, Al, 79
Gowan, Gary, 80
Gravatt, Morrie, 44, 50, 51
Graves, Tim, 80
Gray, Frank and Laurabelle, 52–53
Green, Tammie, 94–95
Griffith, Milt, *54*
Grimes, A. Danner, 38, 42, 43, 47
Grimes, Jo Ann, 47
Grimes, Oscar, 47, 51–52
Grimes Walker, Danna Sue, 43–44
Grout, Dick, 27, 31
Grout, Jenny, 45
Grubb, Howard, 60–61
Guadagnino, Kathy Baker, 84–85
Guild, Jack, 31
Gunderson (Carner), JoAnne, 49–50
Gwin, Ted, 45
Gwinnup, Harry, 15, 24

H

Hagen, Walter, *23*
Haisten, Bill, 86, 88, 90
Hammons, John Q., 94
Hanneman, Candy, 86
Hannigan, Frank, 20
Hannon, E. F., 11
Hanson, Tracy, 94
Hartzell, Bob, 32
Haskell, Coburn, 13
Hayes, Jim, 78
Haynie, Sandra, 49
Heckenkemper, Randy, 75
Heimbach, Gary, *103*
Helmersson, Filippa, 86
Henry, Clay, 71–72, 75, 76
Heslet, Greta, *104*
Higgins, Bob, 30–31
Higgins, Joan, 101
Hill, Carolyn, 84
Hill, Opal, 20
Hillcrest Country Club, 57
Hillcrest Medical Center, 9
Hines, David, 60
Hirsch, Manuel, 12
Hixon, George, 58, 60
Hobbs, Michael, *114*
Hogan, Ben, 22, 37, *38*, 44
Holley, Grant, *106*
Holley, Greg, 7
Honn, Donald, *56*, 57, 60–62
Hoover, John, 90
Hope, Bob, 39, 44
Hopkins, Angie, 84
Hotz, Mabel, 47
Houck, A. C., 11
Hughett, Mike, 77–78
Hullett, Jamie, 95
Hutchison, Jock, 26

I

ice storm (2007), 97–99
Indian Hills Country Club, 29, 31, 48
Ingram, Jack, 78
Inkster, Juli, 93
Irwin, Rob, 7

J

Jackson, Art, 22, 30
Janssen, Mary Patton, 49
January, Don, 71–72, *73*
Johnson, Johnny, 51
Johnson, Mary, *112*
Johnson, Will, *112*
Johnston, George, 30
Johnstone, Ann Casey, 49–50, 59
Jones, Bobby, 19, 20, 37
Jones, Morgan, 40
Jones, Rees, 104
Jones, Rosie, 90
Justice, Ab, 52

K

Kane, Lorie, 94
Kauffman, Earl, 42
Kellough, R. W., 11
Kelsey, Dana, 27
Kemp, E. Rogers, 11, 27
Kendall College, 15. *See also* Tulsa, University of
Kennedy, Agnes, 11, 22
Kennedy, Ann, 11, 49
Kennedy Golf Course, 29, *31*, *32*, 53
Kennedy, James, 11, 13, 16, 22–24, 27, 55
Kennedy, Lee, 11
Kennedy, Dr. Samuel Grant, *10*, 11, 22, 27, 35, 42–43, 79
Kennedy, Samuel Grant, Jr., 11, 30
Kenney, Bob, 7
Kensler, Tom, 78
Kerr, Christie, 95
King, Jim, 7, 14
King, Lou, 70
Klein, John, 85, 90
Koppits, Rinda, 63
Kreager, Jill, 48
Kung, Candie, 95
Kupke, Tom and Biddy, *115*

L

Ladies Professional Golf Association, 7, 83, 85, 87–88, 93
Laffoon, Ky, 39
Laitenen, Niina, 85
Lake, Marion Turpin, 29
Lakeside Country Club, 14
Lampton, Tim, 93
Lang, Diane, 100–102, *103*
Langford, William M., 17
LaPlante, Roger, *54*
Lawson, Fred, 52
Leovy, F. A., 11, 27
Leroux, Ed, 42, 64
Leslie, Tim, 7, 69, 76
Lincoln Park Golf Course, 22, 30
Linihan, Richard, 72
Little, Lawson, 32
Lobaugh, Tom, 47, 48, 53, 62, 68
Lofgren, E. M. "Pete," *54*
Lopez, Nancy, 83, 89
Lortondale, 61
Lukken-Peterson, Adele, 85
Lutz, Fred, 78

M

MacGregor Golf, 13
Mahoney, John, 38
Malloy, Jack, 30
Marks, Suzy, 49
Martin, L. J., 11
Mase, Bob, 78
Masters Golf Tournament, 32, 50
Maxwell, Perry, 34
Mayo, James M., 33, 45
McAlester (Okla.), 60
McAlester Country Club, 41
McClure, Mack, 51
McFarlin, Kim, 84
McGee, Terry, 97
McGurn, Boodie, 101
McIntire, Barbara, 49
McNamara, Dale Fleming, 7, 48, 50, 63, 83–85, 87, 90
McNamara, Melissa, 88, 89
McNeal, Scott, *113*
McSpaden, Harold "Jug," 30–31, 39–42, 50
McPartland, Bill, 51
Meadowbrook Country Club, 60–61

Mehlhorn, William E. "Bill," 21–23, 24, 27
Melton, Walt, 52
Memorial Day weekend flood, 71
Miegs, Roy, 69–70
Miller, Ruth White, 59
Minnich, Craig, 68
Mitchell, John, 11
Mockett, Cathy, 85
Mohawk Park Golf Course, 29, 33
Mohler, Noreen, 101
Moody, Orville, 71
Moore, C. F., 15
Moore, Frank L., 11–12
Moreau, T. J., 17
Morrish, Jay, 21, *74*, 75–76, 83
Morse, Linda Melton, 48, 63
Moss, Flint, 21
Mueller, Eric, 7, 77–78, 80
Mueller, F. P. "Dude," *64*
Mundis, Joe, 102
Murdock, F. Lee, 39–40, 53–54, 64, 79
Murphy, Bob, 60
Murray, Gov. William H., 30
Muskogee (city), 9, 14, 60
Muskogee Town and Country Club, 14, 15

N

National Association of Intercollegiate Athletics, 84
National College Athletic Association Women's Fall Preview, 85
National Collegiate Athletic Association Division I Women's Golf Championship, 84–86
Neal, Harold, 7, 71, 76, 88
Nelson, Byron, 39–42, 44
Nichols, Jimmy, 41
Nichols, William, 14, 27
Nick, Joe, 80
Nicklaus, Jack, 27
Normile, John, 61
Norville, Richard, 58

O

Oaks (Oakhurst) Country Club, 21, 29
Octagon, 94
Oglesby, Robert, 12
O'Kane, Dan, 85, 87–88, 95
Oklahoma, University of, 32, 52
Oklahoma City, 14, 48
Oklahoma Golf Association, 14, 38
Oklahoma Junior Girls championship, 47–49
Oklahoma Men's Amateur, 15, 19, 23–24, 51–52, 60, 67, 77
Oklahoma Open, 14–15, 23–24, 27, 30–31, 32, 44, 51, 60
Oklahoma State University (Oklahoma A&M), 52, 58, 68, 85
Oklahoma women's amateur championship, 45, 48, 63, 84
Oral Roberts University, 68, 77
Osage County, 11, 38, 43
Osage Hills Apartments, 76, 97
Osage Indians, 11, 38

P

Pak, Se Ri, 94
Palmer, Johnny, 51
Palmers, Sandra, 59
Pardue, Dorothy Klotz, 29–30
Park, Gloria, 89–90, 93
Park, Grace, 85–86
Parker, Bill, 52
Perkins, Lilian, 26
Perry, E. R., 12, 15
Perry, Mike, 84
Pershing, Gen. John J., 25
Pertierra, Vicky, 101
Phillips, Buddy, 70
Phillips, Waite, 34–35
Pilot, Claudia, 101
Pine Valley, New Jersey, 33
Pittman, Jerry, 52
Pitts, Ann, 85
Polm, Brian, *114*
Prammanasudh, Stacy, 84–85, 89, *90*, 95
Pringle, Dick, 41
Professional Golfers' Association, 7, 70
Professional Golfers' Association Championship, 22, 37, 70
Professional Golfers' Association Senior Tour, 70
Puckett, Robyn, 101

Q

Quail Creek Golf & Country Club, 78, 100

R

Rampelberger, Susan, 101
Ransom, Grace, 26
Rawlinson, Nancy, 47
Ray, Ted, 26
Redman, Susie, 89
Reeder, C. L., 11
Reynolds, Cathy, 9
Richard, Tanna Lee, 101
Ridgeway, Angie, 89
Riegel, Robert "Skee," 50–51
Riggin, T. H., 54–55, 57, 64
Robbins, Fred, 64
Robbins, Kelly, 84, 89, *91*
Robertson, Henry, 30
Rodolf, Frank, 33, 34–35
Rodricks, Mrs. Dan, 55
Rogers, E. J., 31
Rogers, Will, 9, 30
Roop, Gene, 69
Rosales, Jennifer, 85
Rose, Harold, 11
Russell, Tom, *74, 114*
Ryan, Bob, 58–59
Ryan, Don, 62
Ryder Cup, 22, 51

S

Saint John Medical Center, 25
Sander, Anne, 100
Sanders, Toby, 69–70
Sarazen, Gene, *23*, 27
Savage, Irma, 47
Schneiter, George, 39, *40*, 41
Schultz, Anna, 101
Scott, Maggie, 101
Scranton, Nancy, 89
Seibert, Joe, 62
Senior PGA Tour Championship, 88
Shawnee (Okla.), 14
Shawnee-on-the-Delaware, Pennsylvania, 21
Shoemaker, Forrest, Jr., 7, 48, 61–62, 64, 69, 76, 83
Silvestrone, Art, 71–72
Sisemore, Paul, 7
Skala, Carol Jo, 59
slot machines, 33, 38
Smith, Bill, 51
Smith, Craig, 102
Smith, Dr. Mike, 7
Snead, Sam, 37, 38, 40–42, 44, 51
Sorenson, Carol, 49
Sorenstam, Annika, *88*, 89, 93–94
Southern California, University of, 85
Southern Hills Country Club, 34–35, 40, 44, 45, 59, 60, 88, 102
Southwestern Invitational (Tulsa Open), 40, 44
Spartan School of Aeronautics, 37
Spuzich, Sandra, 50, 59
Stanley, C. Page, 64
Stecher, Steve, 7, 95
Steel, J. A., 12
Steen, A. B., 73, 105
Stephenson, Jan, 89
Stillwater Country Club, 68

Stodghill, Alex, *114*
Stone, Beth, 48
Strege, John, 37
Streit, Marlene, 100
Stubblefield, Cleve, 7, 79, 88
Stucker, E. L., 62
Sturm's Statehood Magazine, 10
Sykes, Dan, 72

T

Taylor, Matt, 11
Teske, Rachel, 89–90
The Dogs, 52–53
Thompson, Carole Semple, 100–101
Thompson, David, 7, 67, 69, 70, 76, *112*
Thompson (Rogers), Jeannie, 48, 49, 58–59
Thomson, Peter, 72
Tillinghast, A. W., *18*, 19–21, 22, 62–63, 75–76, *82*, 83, *100*, 104
Tillinghast Association, 7
Tillinghouse, 80, *81*, *116*
Toscano, Harry, Jr., 58–59
Trans-Mississippi Golf Association, 29, 48, 50, 58–59
Tucker, Grace (Mother), 76
Tulsa, University of, 15, 31–32, 50, 51, 68, 70, 83–86
Tulsa Club, 34–35
Tulsa Country Club (original), 9–10
Tulsa Country Club Dixieland Swing Beatdown Philharmonic Jazz Orchestra, 64
Tulsa District Golf Association, 38
Tulsa Fire Department, *16*
Turner, John, 42, 45
Turnesa, Joe, *23*
Twin Hills Country Club, 30, 45, 51, 60
Tyrell, H. C., 11
Tyson, Miriam Burns Horn, 29

U

Unruh, Jim, 7, 24, 42, 62–63, 64, 77, *105*
Unruh, Paula, *105*
U.S. Girls Junior Championship, 49, 95
U.S. Golf Association, 7, 31, 37, 47
U.S. Men's Amateur, 32, 45
U.S. Open, 7, 9, 22, 50, 70, 88
U.S. Senior Women's Amateur, 100–104
U.S. Women's Amateur, 49–50, 100

V

Vaananen, Paul, 64
Valdez, Louis and Ernestine, 62
Van Zandt, Logan, 30–31
Vardon, Harry, 26
Vare, Glenna Collett, 29
Vollstedt, Linda, 86
Von Glahn, Bill, 88

W

Walker, Danna Sue Grimes, 7, 43–44
Walker Cup, 32, 33, 50, 58
Wallace, Joyce, 30, 45, 49
Waller, Megan, 84
Walser, Joe, Jr., 51–52
Waltrous, Al, *23*
Ward, Wendy, 89–90
Warson Country Club, 58
Webb, Karrie, 89, *91*, 94–95
Weder, Maggie, 101
Weese, Ron, 7
Weese, Sonya, 7, 100, 102, *103*
Weinshilboum, Charles, 60
Weiss, Karen, 9
Western Open, 22
Whiskey Cup, The, *72*
White, P. J., 11
Whitehead, Barb, 85
Whitehead, George, 39

Wichita Country Club, 59
Wiesner, Toni, 101–102
Wilkerson, Terry, 68
Williams, Paul, 7
Williams, Rex J., 78
Williams Companies, 68, 85, 88, 93–94
Williams LPGA Championship, 88, 93–94
Williams LPGA Pro-Am, 85–87
Williamson, G. T., 11, 12
Williford, Margaret, 48, 63
Wilson, Dylan, *106*
Winters, John, 31
Wolfe, Rick, 20
Women's Oklahoma Golf Association, 7, 26, 47, 84
Woods, L. C. "Bud," 54
Word, Bailey, *73*, *75*, *77*
Wotherspoon, Bill, 39
Wrightsman, Charles J., 11, 12

Y

Young, Leonard, 52
Yust, J. H., 12

ABOUT THE AUTHOR

Randy Krehbiel is an Oklahoma native and a Tulsan since 1979. As a reporter for the *Tulsa World*, he has written about a wide range of subjects, from college football and basketball to politics and history. His work has appeared in numerous magazines, and he is the author of *Tulsa's Daily World: The Story of a Newspaper and Its Town* and *Little Bighorn*.

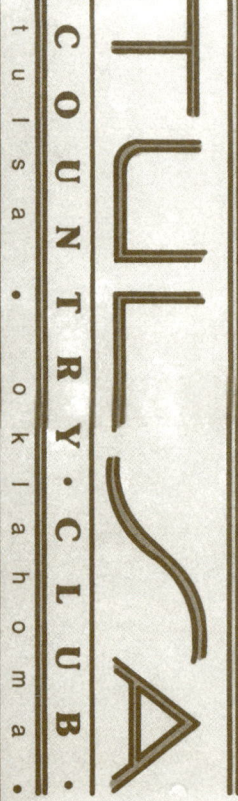

LANDSCAPE PLANTING PLAN FOR

TULSA COUNTRY CLUB

· tulsa · oklahoma ·

Golf Course Remodel By:

Jay Morrish and Associates, Ltd.
10820 East 45th Street   Suite 101
Tulsa, OK 74146   918-665-2937

Landscape Master Plan By:

PLANNING DESIGN GROUP
Land Planning/Golf Course Architecture/Landscape Architecture
9155 East 51st Street, Suite 105, Tulsa, Oklahoma 74145 918-628-1255

LEGEND

- Acer rubrum 'October Glory'
  October Glory Red Maple
- Cedrus deodara (150 yd. Markers)
  Deodar Cedar
- Cercis canadensis
  Redbud
- Fraxinus americana 'Autumn Purple'
  Autumn Purple White Ash
- Pinus nigra
  Austrian Pine
- Pyrus calleryana
  Bradford Pear
- Quercus Spp. rubra, shumardi, nigra
  Northern Red Oak, Shumard Oak, Water Oak